15¢

Dorothy R. Morrill.
Dec. 1910 —

ADVENTURES IN HOME-MAKING

ADVENTURES IN HOME-MAKING

ROBERT AND
ELIZABETH
SHACKLETON

ILLUSTRATED WITH MANY PHOTOGRAPHS

NEW YORK
JOHN LANE COMPANY
MCMX

PUBLISHERS PRINTING COMPANY, New York

CONTENTS

[9]

LIST OF ILLUSTRATIONS

LIST OF ILLUSTRATIONS

ADVENTURES IN HOME-MAKING

CHAPTER I

THE FINDING OF A HOME

WHEN we looked over the house, wondering whether we should make it our home, it was clear that it would demand both faith and works: a very strong faith and a great deal of work. But also, from the first, it was evident—and that was the saving grace of it all —that there were possibilities. "Hope told a flattering tale." We took the house. We planned, we contrived, we visualized. And the substance of things hoped for became gradually clear, and the evidence of things not seen was justified.

It was all so delightfully worth while! We had lived the renter's existence. We had learned the difficulty of looking into home-making happiness through another man's house. Now we were to try with our own.

To be a renter and to have ideas is discouraging. For, properly to live, one must be ready to adapt, to change, to improve; and one naturally hesitates to spend much money on another's property. Nor, even if a tenant should so spend, is there any certainty that the owner would consider an improvement an improvement. No man is a hero to his landlord.

It was doubtless out of unhappy experience that the old-time writer set down that ownership can make a bare rock into a paradise, whereas a rented paradise is likely to decline into bareness.

In picking out a home for ownership and afterward in altering, outfitting, and furnishing it, it is not only one's own judgment that should be followed but one's own personality, one's own individuality. Throughout, let Individuality be the household god. Noses were not given us to be led by; each man should follow his own.

The principles that govern good looks, attractiveness, fitness, are the same whether a house is owned or rented, the same whether a

house represents millions or thousands or hundreds.   Good taste is the same everywhere.
Convenience is the same.   Good looks are the same.

It was on a day in the late fall that we set
forth on our quest of a home.   We had decided
that the home should be suburban.   Our aim,
indeed, was at that delightful desideratum, a
home of accessible seclusion; a home where we
should have privacy and isolation, yet where we
should, at the same time, be in easy touch with
our friends, and whence we could readily go to
the near-by city, whether by day or night.
Gibbon loved to write that his home gave him
scenery, seclusion, and companionship—thus
conjuring up a charming picture.

We drove along attractive roads, we made
trips by rail to this or that suburban point, we
inquired freely, we watched for signs of "For
Sale."

Very early we realized that our search should
be confined within certain limits, and those
limits were still more narrowed by observation.

Necessarily, one must choose a home not too
inconveniently situated for the demands of one's
business.   But it is seldom that this means the

choice of a situation unattractive, unpleasing, or prosaic. Rather than yield to such a condition, look a little longer till you find business convenience and general attractiveness combined. And a little inconvenience, which after all will probably be but temporary, is well borne for the sake of making one's home in admirable surroundings.

And one should always and heedfully choose where there is promise that the neighbors will be people not uncongenial, and where there is every reason to expect that the houses will be at least as good as his own; if there is to be a difference, let them be better. And if, as is likely enough, such a neighborhood may be prohibitively expensive, go in the line in which that neighborhood gives promise of advancing. Go bravely among the pioneers, and the mountain will soon reach to Mahomet. Do not, tempted by cheapness, go into an inferior neighborhood or in a wrong direction. Within reasonable limits a home-seeker can usually get what he wants where he wants it. Hitch your wagon to a suburban star!

Our inquiries taught us many curious facts. One, which seems to set arithmetic at defiance, is that it is as cheap to buy a place of ten acres as of five. For when a place is of the size of ten acres or more the house is likely to be thrown in, or at least considered as a quite negligible feature, whereas, with five acres or less, the house will be figured at its full value.

This applies, of course, to houses that are not new. For any one whose resources are limited it is better to buy than to build, and better to buy an old house than a new, paying no attention to the cynically humorous averment that old houses mended cost little less than new before they're ended, for this need not at all be the case. It certainly will not be the case if the house has been wisely chosen.

Beginning our quest of a home, we carefully sought out house after house in search of the ideal that we were confident was somewhere to be found. But we well knew that the ideal was likely to be an ideal well disguised; and it is fortunate that it is so, else the ideals would all too soon be seized upon by others.

One house that we saw appealed to us very strongly. It long antedated the Revolution, and was of superb beauty in proportion and design, being, indeed, one of the most beautiful

Colonial houses in any of the Northern States. Its interior was of spacious charm, with wealth of paneling, wainscoting, and window-seats.

There was reason to think it could be reasonably bought; but we did not buy, for a railroad track ran near the house, giving noise and smoke, and we discovered that the railroad company had purchased heavily of land, giving threatening possibilities of switch yards and factories. And, too, though the neighborhood was good, with fine people and fine houses, there was that intangible something in the air which gave warning that the residential climax had been reached. We could not look on it as a place with a future. We felt that we must have something whose value should rise as the mortgage should fall. That the house was in evil case as regarded repairs was not so bad. If the price were right it would be a labor of love to rejuvenate and restore so much beauty.

It is well to be romantic in the buying of a home, for to secure one's own home is, rightly considered, one of the most romantic things in life. But, unless one chances to be independently rich, romance must needs be tempered by practicality. In buying a home there must be an eye on the future as well as the present, for at any time, on account of changes in business, or, perhaps, from sickness or disaster, a sale may be imperative—and then romance looms low. A friend put fifteen thousand dollars into a home on a romantic island. It was delightful. But only a year later he needed to sell, and found that nobody but himself cared fifteen thousand dollars for the whole island. That unsalable island may stand as a warning for discretion, for financial wariness. But wariness need not mean stinginess. It may, on the contrary, mean a higher preliminary cost. The important thing is the proper appreciation of "the present value of a distant advantage," to use one of Macaulay's happy phrases.

The development of a city or a suburb is one of fact and not of theory. Theory may point in one direction as the best line of progress; fact may point in another. The theory may be well based, too; it may have been mere chance or whim that directed the fact contrariwise. But do not quarrel with facts. Do not buy to prop a falling neighborhood or to accelerate one whose impetus has ceased. At the same time one should not be overcautious. There are times when it is both pleasant and profitable to yield to an impulse.

A dweller in one of our Western cities found his health failing and, though far from wealthy, began to dream of retiring for the rest of his days. He was driving aimlessly one afternoon in the outskirts of the town. He drew up in front of a tiny old farmhouse to ask as to the direction of a neat old woman who was leaning against the rose-covered gate. He looked weary, and she asked him inside to rest. He was fascinated by the shiny neatness, the immaculateness of everything, the calico-covered chairs, the log-cabin quilt on the high-piled bed.

"How much will you take to move out and leave me everything just as it is?" he asked.

She called "Father," there were a few minutes of cautious sibilation, then: "Two thousand dollars."

The next day he wrote out a check, and the day after that he was enjoying his rest-place in the country.

In our own case, the house-search was not so swiftly over; and yet it took but the spare time of a few weeks in all, for it was followed with definite purpose. We soon narrowed the possibilities, for our own ideas and needs, to a strip of territory bordering the railroad we had chosen. This strip gave promise of building up admirably, and yet was just beyond the zone of great expense.

Within that area every buyable house was carefully examined. There was no great number, for it was a neighborhood principally of large landholders, who lived on their own property and controlled its splitting up. Resident landholders stand for safety of development. They are bulwarks against unattractive allotments. They stand for the permanency of present attractiveness.

One of the delightful conceits of the always delightful George William Curtis was that every man may be in essence the owner of the land he sees, even though he actually owns not a foot of it, for he may enjoy the air, the view, the beauty, the charm, as keenly as the very landowner himself. There is so much of truth in this, in the spirit in which Curtis meant it, that one does not need to point out any fallacy from another standpoint. And, there being so much of truth in it, it follows that a buyer of land is buying not only within the limits set down in his own title-deeds, but all the places that are in view from his own. If they are beautiful, attractive, fine, it is so much fineness, attractiveness, beauty, taken into his own possession; if they are the opposite of beauty, he is paying his money for ugliness. Look with solicitude, therefore, to the land about you; look not only to its present condition, but to its possibilities, judging from the character of the owners and the probable development of the neighborhood.

One should have in mind, from the beginning, at least a general idea of the type of house desired. Our own taste runs to the old-fashioned, and within the region there were several places that it was possible to secure. It is not that we hold the old-fashioned to be better than the new, but always in such a matter there must be individual taste, and our own personal taste led in the direction of the stately architecture of the American past, with its fine and simple lines. But the main thing is to have a home of beauty, for beauty is always its own sufficient justification and is independent of periods and years, although it is well to learn that some periods are fecund of beauty and others are not.

THE FINDING OF A HOME

One place was good, but too exposed to the north wind, without sheltering trees or shade of any kind. Another tempted, but there was no certainty of good water supply, even with the expedient of a windmill. The water used was from a brook into which went the drainage of one or two houses upstream. Another was attractive except that the barn was offensively in front of it, and we felt no desire to be at the expense of tearing the barn down and building another. Others were too far from railway station or post-office.

At the same time we were prepared to put up, if necessary, with quite a degree of inconvenience for the sake of price, and in view of anticipative accruing advantages of the near future. The moment that one demands all conveniences he should be ready to pay an inconvenient price.

A house that much attracted us was charmingly situated in a valley; but our second visit to it was in the early evening of a dampish day and we found that rising mist had enveloped it, although the land above was clear and free. One house, otherwise attractive, was barred by factory chimneys that showed up gauntly in the middle distance; and we gave that vicinage a wide berth, for one factory breeds another.

We found a charming old house, all of stone, set upon a slope and shaded by a highly pictorial pine. Although it had no door in its long and otherwise well-proportioned front, one of its windows could be made into a door with little consequent alteration of the interior. A disfigurement was a scraggly bit of fencing that ran close in front of the house, separating it from the field, but in a few minutes this could be torn down, adding materially to the air of dignity. A few great, old beams were still in the ceilings, and with more beams and with paneled oak there could have been great effectiveness. The place, however, was too far from a railway station and altogether away from a trolley, and furthermore there was not a sufficiently good view to make one put up with the drawbacks.

Another house had a good front, except that the first floor was too high up on account of a sharp ascent, and that the too-high appearance of the house was accented by a peak between two dormers. By taking off the peak, however, and continuing the dormered roof line, with the addition of a dormer between the two already there, a vital improvement would be made and the apparent height reduced. Then, below, a well-filled-in terrace would relieve the too-high aspect of the first floor. But, in this case, the price was too high to permit of the additional cost of needful alterations.

Many a house, not desirable as it stands, may be made possible. It isn't what a house is that counts: it is what it may be made.

Most people, in buying, give a mortgage for part of the price. A man who is ready to pay forty dollars a month rent is usually ready to pay, on a home investment, at the rate of fifty dollars or more when full ownership is the goal. One should not figure on whether he is able to assume a debt of four thousand, eight thousand, fifteen thousand dollars, but whether he is in a position to face periodical payments that will gradually reduce that debt. This idea, practically realized, at once simplifies the situation.

It is even simpler than this. There is usually a considerable first payment made, and then, although in strictness a man is still paying directly or indirectly on the whole amount of the investment, he is facing actual payment of interest on a smaller and steadily-decreasing sum.

His interest is like a rent—only that he finds himself paying far less than the sum for which he could rent such a property.

And always there is the asset of the property itself, which, if the chooser has been fortunate, is of a value steadily increasing. Sickness and disaster may come, but from disaster and sickness even the renter is not free.

Take, as an illustration, an entirely supposititious case, but such an one as often happens. A man buys an eight-thousand-dollar place. It goes up to a ten-thousand value, while his mortgage, beginning at, say, six, is reduced to five. Interest and taxes and repairs together then will amount to not over thirty dollars a month for a ten-thousand-dollar property. And in a few years the value may go to twelve thousand, while the mortgage gets down to three. Isn't it worth trying for?

We found that winter or late fall is the best time to examine property, for, with the leaves stripped from the trees, all barenesses and disadvantages of surroundings come into view. Then, too, is the time to see if roads are impassable and cellars puddly. In one fine house, a former Governor's home, we found chopping-block and milk-cans bobbing about in three feet of water. If one goes house-seeking in the suburbs in the apple-blossom season every prospect pleases.

One house had a view hemmed in by softly-rising slopes. It was of stone, and well proportioned. Its face was toward the view, and its back, with projecting kitchen, was frankly toward the highway. Still, retaining the porch and the view, it was clear that the back of the house should be made its front, or at least its mode of approach. A kitchen should be built at one end. Between the house and the road, a garden suggested itself in place of the cabbage field that was there, and it was clear that a towering hedge should be reduced to a less forbidding height.

Another house not far away also presented temptations, for it was near a railroad station, had good water supply, and was well built. It was, however, too tall for its width, and imperatively needed, from our standpoint, one more room on the ground floor. Its dormerless roof, too—it was the kind of house that needs dormers—would require reconstruction on a different angle before dormers could be possible.

Inside, the stair was a disadvantage, because it came down between walls right at the front door, without a hall. All these disadvantages could be overcome by alterations, were the price sufficiently tempting. If one should save an extra thousand on price he could well afford to put it on improvements.

Always, one should look for convenience of churches and schools and markets, for these are points that are bound to be considered if it should ever be desired to sell. One of the old-fashioned English landscape gardeners wrote, long ago, that a church spire is indispensable " in an elegant landscape," and this elegant reason may be added to reasons utilitarian.

One cool day in early winter we came to a house on a hillside. We had seen other houses on hillsides, but this was different.

In the first place it was homelier. Frankly, it was ugly. And yet it was evident that there were possibilities. It was, as a matter of fact, the sought-for ideal—but it was an ideal well disguised!

It looked like nothing else than an elongated boarding house. The center was the part with merit, and this was of the old-fashioned style of

THE HOUSE AS WE FOUND IT

(For the house, as altered and completed, see page 346)

architecture that we loved; but this central portion almost failed to attract attention on account of the aggressive ugliness of the wings. And never was there a greater misuse of the word. Wings are supposed to be, in their very essence, things of beauty, of airiness, of charm; yet here were wings that were heavy, inharmonious, awkward, unsightly.

It was a larger house than we had looked for, but that did not greatly trouble us, for we knew that it would be far easier to use space generously than to build new space upon too-cramped quarters.

From the front of the house there was a delectable and widespreading view of miles and miles of land most charmingly rolling and with masses and clumps of trees. Indeed, looking in any direction there was charm. And yet the house was less than fourteen miles from the city hall of the third city in the country, but just outside of the city limits, and was in a region of well-made macadam roads—this matter of roads being one of the most vital of all the questions to be considered by the intending rural dweller.

The frontage was delightfully toward the

southeast. There was no factory chimney in sight; no factory within miles. There were no disagreeable neighbors. A railway station was accessible; a trolley was even a little nearer. And a trolley is often a great convenience for a suburbanite. The house had running water. It was above the rising of the evening mists. It was in the territory where we wished to settle. It was within three miles of a public library, and much nearer to schools and churches. It was shaded and sheltered by trees, and was of a seclusion as great as could be wished for by any but those who long for a lodge in a vast wilderness. And yet this seclusion was so accessible!

But the outward ugliness gave pause. A quarter of a century ago the appearance of the house, built of stone, had been marred to apparent hopelessness by these ugly wooden wings, impossibly gabled, and by crenelations of galvanized iron along the ridges.

We went over the problem. Here were things to be done. Here were lines to be altered, unsightly things to be made sightly. But, after all, it was clear that it would be cheaper to alter what was in position than to take some building which would at once require additions. And it would be far cheaper than to build a new house from the ground up.

The price—and we mention it so as to make this book practical, and to show that we are writing of sums not beyond the great majority of Americans—was ten thousand dollars, including the house and barns and eleven acres; and we were at liberty to leave a very considerable part on mortgage, at five per cent, if we desired. The place was in the heart of a tract of some few hundred acres that was intended, by the owner, to be opened up as a residence park, in parcels of not less than three acres; and, indeed, this provision and protective provisions regarding things commonly considered to be nuisances, were to go into the deed. This was the only old house on the tract. All others were to be built new. It seemed an ideal opportunity.

We took the house; to have and to hold, for better, for worse. We planned, we contrived, we visualized. And we found ourselves faced formally with a multitude of problems of alteration and adaptation, outdoors and in—we were, in truth, to find it a matter of faith and works.

CHAPTER II

THE PLANNING

A ND so we were adventuring for a home: venturing and adventuring. And we were not to build a chateau in Spain but to alter an American house on an American hillside.

It was not a slight thing that we were facing. We were to make a home out of unpromising materials; we were to alter and transform from unattractiveness; and we were to do it with constant watchfulness of expense.

On every hand there were things that needed changing, altering, remedying. But on every hand there were such possibilities!

The house was two stories and a garret in height. It had a frontage of sixty-six feet and yet, although larger than we really needed or had looked for, it was not nearly so large in reality as this frontage would imply, because, to take full advantage of the view, it had been made wide and shallow instead of narrow and deep. It had a broad frontage of prospect-commanding windows, and yet, except in the wings, was a house of only one-room depth. And it was better for us that the house was too large rather than too small if it had to be one or the other. It is easier to take down than to build; easier to make a room by destroying a partition than by constructing a wing.

Behind the house, toward the north, was a fine wind-break of thirty-year-old hemlock spruce; these dark green trees at once summoning up the picture of a white house set in front of them, though the house as we first saw it was of a disheartening drab.

Behind the wind-break there was a gentle rise, for the house was under the lee of the crest and was thus further protected from the cold from the northward; but in front of the house, and at either side, the land dropped away in easy slopes, the site having been admirably chosen by the pre-Revolutionary home-maker who built the solid central portion that had stood for so many years.

We first saw the house in winter. It was unoccupied and had been so for months, and it had throughout a musty chill. The windows

3   [33]

were tight-shuttered with the solid, paneled shutters typical of Eastern Pennsylvania, and by match-light we looked at the tiny bedrooms, the impossible main stair, the rusted-out furnace in the cellar, the awkward dining-room, the electric wiring which clung to every ceiling in unsightly wooden channels. But even in that first brief look we saw that there were good points also and that, better than this, there was the pleasing possibility of many a good point more.

That first visit, made as it was toward the close of a gloomy winter's day, really decided us. But, to make sure that it was not over-enthusiasm, we went again, and the second visit was conclusive.

There was much to be done, very much to be done, outdoors and in. That much was clear. But the idea strongly impressed itself on us that not only the man who alters but the man who builds a house has many things to do both outdoors and in. Indeed, it is not often enough considered that, by the side of the difficulties that face a house builder, those of a house alterer do not seem so hopelessly formidable, after all.

THE PLANNING

The house actually in our possession, we made a brief survey of what was to be done.

About the grounds there was a litter of rubbish and stone and stumps and logs. Here and there was a ditch that needed filling. Much fencing was necessary. What ought to be lawn was a medley of shrubs. But the shrubs were rare and fine; there were more than a hundred large trees; there was a splendid spring; there were serviceable barns; there was the noble view; and the cedar-bordered road below us had the association, fascinating to us, that over a long part of it Washington marched on his way to the battle of Germantown.

The outward aspect of the house itself was to be transformed, and in the interior it was clear that there were myriad things to do. Almost from the first we lived in the house, for it is essential to be on hand and in personal touch with alteration work if the result is to be such as will represent one's personal ideas and dreams, one's personal tastes, opinions, beliefs, one's articles of faith in decoration.

Theoretically, one should merely have to walk through an old place, as did Sir Francis and Captain Strong through the long-unoccupied Clavering House, settling each room with a word and then driving unconcernedly away, but that is a trifle too cavalier for ordinary circumstances. The planning of alterations and adaptations is a cogitative task.

We moved in as soon as two or three rooms were ready; and as the house was dry and habitable there was no hardship about it and only some degree of inconvenience—inconvenience amply offset by advantages. Our furniture came by freight, in boxes and crates, and most of it remained in its boxed condition till the proper rooms were ready for it and meanwhile was piled in corners where it would be least in the way.

In the main, we proposed to have all the important rooms altered and completed to accord with our ideas before taking up any of the exterior alterations, except such as were directly connected with this inside work. One side of the house would be altered when doing the dining-room, and the front would be touched, on account of windows, in doing the library, but in neither case would there be any more done with the exterior than would guarantee the rooms from being interfered with later.

THE PLANNING

The final work of all was to be the complete alteration of the entire front, but this was to affect nothing of the interior except a mere trifle in one wing and two unimportant rooms in the garret.

Our aim was at simplicity and spaciousness. The house had been largely cut up into tiny and insignificant rooms and these insignificant and tiny rooms were to go. We knew it to be axiomatic that when a house is altered it is altered to give more rooms; the exceptions only make the rule more marked. But from the beginning our purpose was the uncustomary one. In the first place, we did not need more rooms, as the house was larger than we had expected to take, but even before finding the particular house we had decided that the number of rooms was to be freely sacrificed to size should it be needful from our standard.

There is keen pleasure in carrying out a home ideal without considering what people call practical considerations—as if anything could be practical that conflicts with an ideal! It is strange that many a man, who will freely spend money in traveling to look at the beautiful and attractive things of the world, will grudge the spending of money to make the house he lives in attractive and beautiful unless he can see definite utilitarianism in it. Eden Philpotts, writing of his own home, described it as "hideous without ceasing, from doorstep to chimney," yet the thought of making an attractive home did not appeal to him; he merely hoped to hide his house's ugliness with vines!

At the very beginning of our campaign of alteration it was clear that there must be decided diminution of doors, of partitions, of staircases. Ingenuity had been so taxed with surplusage of outside doors alone that there were actually eight! Stairs went up in such haphazard redundancy that there were four from the cellars alone! Wherever you wanted to step outside, there was a door; wherever you wished to go aloft or below, there was a stair! And as to partitions, it was as if the life principle of our predecessor in ownership had been that two rooms are better than one.

All of which shows that one man's originality is not another man's originality, and that each man should plan for himself.

It was very shortly after we took the place and began its adaptation that we heard of an old

ONE OF THE ROOMS, AS ALTERED (See ch. vi.)

stone house two miles away, which was shortly to be torn down to be replaced by a large new mansion. We at once went over there, because some things were needed for our own house which it would be quite impossible to obtain satisfactorily of a mill or of a dealer, and we instinctively felt that here was an opportunity.

Nor was the instinct wrong. There were several fine mahogany doors, which we found ourselves coveting to take the place of certain doors of grained pine. "You would like to buy these?" said the man in charge. "You may have them. Otherwise they would all be burned."

There was a beautiful old staircase with charming banisters and mahogany rail, and from the first we had wondered where to find such a stair to take the place of a modern one of hybrid mid-Victorian form. Our own place being old and our furniture old, we needed to restore the appearance of the past; and even for a modern house the stairs that had been put in were hopelessly ugly. And again came the welcome formula: "You wish these banisters and rail? Then you may have them."

There were several charming old, white,

wooden mantel-pieces that to see was to desire, and especially as several originals in our house had been taken out, years ago, and replaced with patterns of oaken ineptitude. There was wealth of narrow cupboard door, those cupboards built beside fireplaces; and we realized that these could be used for paneling. "You wish all these? You may have them. For the new owner wishes everything cleared away."

Demolition was to commence soon, and the superintendent would let us know when to send, for the stairs must remain till tearing down should actually begin.

It was well on in the afternoon, four days later, when he sent word that next day would be the time. A carpenter was at once telephoned and full instructions were given him to go early next morning and take out the stair banisters, newel posts, mantels, and cupboards.

Toward noon, along a delightful hill-and-valley road, past pines and maples and beside a running stream, we drove over, just as a matter of precaution, to see if everything was going on properly, and found that from our standpoint things were going very improperly indeed. For the owner, it appeared, had become angered by

delay and had that morning set twoscore
Italians to work; and all were furiously busy,
with crows and axes, with hammers and bare
hands, spurred on by an imperative foreman,
pulling, ripping, tearing, tossing down a continuous shower of stone and wood. And the
carpenter was not to be found! He had gone
leisurely there; had seen the small Italian
army and the cloud of hurtling débris; and
had gone away, deeming it too late to attempt
rescue.

The case was desperate. The impulse was
to get to work instantly, but there were neither
tools nor laborers to be had. So a hasty return trip was made along the road of pines and
maples and running stream, but this time
without thinking so much of their attractiveness,
to get tools and a helper, for it had become a case
where one man alone could not get things out
quickly enough.

Returning, thus re-enforced, the shower of
stones and plaster was still continuing, the
building was rapidly disappearing; in a few
hours it would be too late to get anything at all.
There was nothing for it but to go right in,
dodging dropping débris.

The staircase was first begun with. Its upper part was already destroyed, but there was enough left for our needs. Then came the newel and turning posts, although there was only time to get up one in its full length, two or three others being uprooted by help of a saw. Cupboard doors were cut from their hinges and carried out over steadily-mounting piles of rubbish. The four mahogany doors on the main floor were secured. Two mantels were wrested from their places, the one on the second story amid a particularly fierce storm of missiles. Now and then something struck us; often we escaped a heavy stone or timber by a mere graze. But there was no time to hesitate for little things like that. And at length we had what we wanted, and heaped it together in a great pile well away from the tumult and the shouting, and left it guarded while a heavy team was secured for carrying it home.

And in all it cost but ten dollars! "The stuff would all have been burned. You are over-paying me," said the man. And, indeed, a great bonfire of wreckage was already blazing.

And to all this there was a diverting sequel. The interloping, machine-made, oak-varnished rails and banisters and mantels that we discarded for the danger-secured loot were in turn destined by us for the fire, but also in turn became as brands plucked from the burning. For a carpenter, setting covetous eyes upon them, declared them to be precisely what he needed for his own lately-purchased house; and he offered, in exchange for them and for some deposed sky-blue tiles, to come after hours and on Saturday afternoons to do all sorts of odd jobs up to the value of fifteen dollars in time; an offer at once closed with, whereupon he carted away our discards as proudly as we had gathered in the others. All of which again points out the eternal truth that all men do not have the same tastes; and what an awkward thing life would be, in a host of ways, if they had!

It must not be thought that such adventures as came in our home-making, such opportune happenings or finds, are at all unusual or impossible for others. The world is full of possibilities. Looking is finding, and we all know that "findings is keepings." Whatever is needed will show up somewhere, somehow; or, if it doesn't, there will be something adequate to take its place. It is not necessary to know in advance where things are to be found. When we took this house we knew we should alter the interpolated main staircase with an old one from somewhere else, but had not the slightest definite reason to suppose that it would be found so quickly or so near.

We needed a base for the sun-dial, and found one thrown away in the tall grass. It had never been used as a base, but it was the precise shape and size needed. A chair needed a rush bottom, and we found that an Italian laborer, mending a wall, understood the rare art of rush-working. One day a pounder was needed for the foundation of a brick pavement; and there, close at hand, was a heavy square of iron made for some unknown purpose of the past. Into a hole in its middle a crowbar fitted, and the pounder was made. One of the happiest finds for this house was a set of old diamond-pane windows, and it was the third time we had had the chance to acquire such things—once from an old house in Cleveland, once from a church being destroyed in the old part of New York City, and, as we were not ready to take them over then, not having a house to build them into or a place to stow them away, here was an accommodating Fate making us still another proffer.

From the first we realized many good points about our house, in addition to its location and its general plan. The roof was good, and the walls were good, and most of the floors were capable of treatment as hardwood.

The proper ideals for a house are appearances, comfort, and health, these three, and for the greatest of these some will choose one and some another. As a matter of fact, they should be held as of equal importance with one another. Each should be kept in the forefront of ambition. Some may say that health ought to be placed first, but—sensible though the idea seems— the man who says he puts health first is almost always, as a matter of fact, seeking an excuse for carelessness. With health, good looks should equally be aimed at. There is no reason why both should not be secured, with comfort and convenience as well. And if good looks can easily be made into beauty and distinction, so much the better.

The desire for a good appearance, for beauty, for a home with an air of distinction, implies a desire to stand deservedly well in the opinion of one's friends and neighbors, the determination to put the best foot foremost; surely an admirable thing, even from the standpoint of the most rigid moralist. What some one has aptly called "common-sense made beautiful" seems to cover the ground of what should be aimed at.

And one should always aim at the things he would aim at if money were not a limiting consideration.

Now, this does not in the least mean that one should ape the wealthy, pretentiously copy the wealthy, pretend to be wealthy, but only that, as the rules of beauty and of health are the same for all, there is no reason why a thousand-dollar house should not be as attractive and as healthful as one which costs fifty or a hundred thousand. Indeed, a simple thing stands a better chance of being in good taste than does a thing of ornateness. The cottages of the European peasantry are often perfect models of good living and good looks.

We did not have an architect for any of the interior work, and would not have had one even for the exterior except from the necessity of having formal itemized specifications drawn up, for the contractor, for the alteration of roof beams and the putting in of tall portico pillars. Nor was this exclusion of the architect primarily from motives of economy; it was because we knew that an altered house must be either one's own or one's architect's and we purposed to have this our own. When there is to be a wide variety of miscellaneous alterations, one to follow another, it is not possible to give the work to an architect unless you wish the completed result to represent him and not yourself. Nor could he have the keen personal interest in such a medley of detail that you yourself have.

It would be difficult to secure any good architect for such a task without paying him, comparatively considered, a great sum; and yet, in the usual architect's office, such work of alteration and adaptation, unless for the house of a multimillionaire, would be looked at half-heartedly and given to some 'prentice hand. Instead of securing an admirable result economically there would be an uncertain result achieved extravagantly.

The expensiveness, indeed, would be about all that could be counted on with certainty. For our own house, the previous owner had himself thought of alterations and had asked an architect to plan and estimate on them. The plan offered did not contemplate any exterior alteration whatever, either on side or front. The changes proposed were positively petty, and the house was to retain all its ugliness outside and a medley of tiny rooms within. Yet the estimate was for fifty-five hundred dollars—more than complete metamorphosis was to cost us.

A friend, owning a house which is worth, as it stands, some three thousand dollars, asked an architect the other day for an estimate for proposed alterations and was faced with a straight ten-thousand-dollar proposition. Nor, when such figures are named, is there any possibility that the architect would go over the many varied details that would arouse the owner's personal interest.

Of course, when a man sees to his own planning it takes time. But isn't it an admirable use for time to spend some of it in securing a distinctive and individual and worth-while home? Nor should it be overlooked that, even if an architect is engaged, the owner is likely to spend about as much time as if he weren't, only the time will go in helpless worrying and watching rather than in getting what he wants.

Looking ahead at all the work that was to be done we did not make the mistake of putting it into the hands of some builder as one contract. A contractor would have felt it necessary to make a blanket bid to cover contingencies. Nor would it have been possible to make any one see the plan with our eyes in its entirety. It would have been simply confusing to go over the minute and myriad details. Work of this kind demands continued personal attention from the originators, and a readiness to meet unexpected problems which are likely at any moment to present themselves. A scheme may at any moment be altered to meet an unanticipated situation. It is possible to visualize a great deal, but it is not possible to visualize every result and every emergency. Work of this sort demands interest of a kind which can not be expected from a contractor any more than from an architect.

But although it would not be wise to put all such alteration work in one contract it would be equally unwise to have it all done on the basis of time and material. There is sure to be less

4

loitering, sure to be fewer accidents and fewer unexpected delays, sure to be fewer days when the workmen sit in the sunshine waiting for lumber, if the houseowner is not to stand the loss. And, therefore, so far as feasible, the work was divided into parts that were taken up separately as we came to them, and contracts were made with carpenter or mason or painter, for a fireplace, a chimney, certain window-frames, altering an end of the house, building bookcases, laying a porch pavement of brick, as these items were approached.

Necessarily, there was considerable that could only be done by day work, and for this we had men whom we deemed trustworthy through our experience with them in contracts, and we always made a point of having the place where they were to work ready and cleared and everything on hand so far as this could be seen to.

Now, stairs, partitions, doors seem to most people as unalterable as the laws of the Medes and Persians, but, in reality, they are easy of demolition and change. So seeming formidable, the tasks are not at all Herculean. Any one taking over a house that some one else built should prepare to face such propositions.

THE FRONT DOOR, AS ALTERED   (See ch. xvii.)

A door in an ordinary partition wall can be taken out and the space covered with lath and plaster so readily that there should be no hesitation in getting at it. It costs little to take out a partition and make two tiny rooms into one of size and dignity. It costs little to take out a stairway and put flooring across the hole. New doors can be cut with little trouble or expense. In our cellar a doorway was needed through a partition wall of solid stone twenty-two inches across, and it was cut, six feet high, and timbers were cemented in place across the top, and the sides were smoothed and plastered, for a cost of just five dollars.

Approached and managed properly the total cost of changes should be much smaller than one would at first deem likely, for many of the most formidable-appearing items ought really to be not formidable at all. But here is an important point. If you have regard for economy make all structural interior alteration—the alterations in floors and walls—before the plastering and painting and decorating are done, for otherwise there will be most of the decorating, painting, and plastering to do over again.

Always, during house alteration, it is necessary

to give thought to everything that is going on, for otherwise some mistake is sure to slip through. A carpenter one day inadvertently sealed up two hammers and a box of nails inside a window-seat.

"I wouldn't 'a' done that if I'd thought," he said, when he suddenly realized what he had done; "but," he added slowly, "a man can't be thinkin' *all* the time."

The houseowner, however, *must* be thinking all the time.

CHAPTER III

BEGINNING WITH THE LIBRARY

IT was with the library that we began; and the library was to occupy the lower floor of the east wing, and it was to be one long room in place of two rooms and a hall, and there were to be many other alterations, including the tearing away of two pair of stairs.

Looking back on it all, it seems as if the two primary ideas we had in mind were that a library should look like a library and that a long room ought to be of practically equal importance at either end.

A library should have shelves and books, or, at least, there should be a place for shelves, and there should be the intention to get the books. There are so-called libraries whose wall-space is so taken up with doors and windows and fireplaces and heavy furniture as to leave no room for shelves. Such rooms may be very attractive, but they should not be called libraries.

[53]

ADVENTURES IN HOME-MAKING

David Copperfield's home at Blunderstone had a rookery without rooks, a pigeon-house without pigeons, and a great dog-kennel without any dog; it needed only a library without books.

The presence of books presupposes that they should be in view. In the early days of books, when each copy represented lavish cost, and when many books were in precious illuminated manuscript, they were kept in covered chests or closed cases, like other costly treasure; and precious rarity is excuse sufficient for such a library of to-day as that of the Vatican, which keeps its books out of sight. But the usual library ought to show its books freely.

Nor should it be overlooked that the appearance of the books themselves, in row after row of soft greens or reds or buckram, is an important factor in the decorative appearance of a room and should add much to the attractiveness. Serried rows of books are such a delight to the eye that one almost finds it in his heart to pardon the men who merely order sufficient well-bound volumes to fill spaces, without regard to titles.

The appearance of a library is much the best

when there is no glass in front of the books. It is hard to make a room look well with case after case glass-fronted. And, too, the absence of doors and glass gives a delightful air of accessibility.

The idea that every long room should have its two ends equally inviting, equally interesting, equally engaging, involves the taking up of a different problem with every room. And yet, broadly speaking, the ways are three: to have a window, or cluster of windows, at each end, with a fireplace midway along the side, as we have seen delightfully done; to have a fireplace at each end, for twin blazes to flicker at each other, as in the banquet-room of Independence Hall and as we remember seeing in one of the charming homes of the Eastern Shore; or to have a fireplace at one end and attractive windows at the other, which was our own choice under our own circumstances.

And this would give admirable advantages. The front end of our library, looking in the ideal direction of the southeast, would have a cluster of windows and a window-seat; and the other end, which was toward the bleakest direction, the northwest, would very properly have neither door nor window, but would have the fireplace.

This was all very well; but it seems rather humorous, looking back at it, that at the time we planned it the very room itself was still to be evolved through elimination and merger, and the fireplace was to be built where there was no fireplace at all, and the cluster of windows was to be procured and set in. And with this absence of what was needful there was a surplusage of what must be discarded.

Had it been necessary to build a wing, a good way would have been to use steel framework and concrete; an admirable method of putting up a fire-proof wing with no unreasonable cost. But, fortunately, we had the wing, and it would be far less costly to make even extensive changes than to build. And that partitions and stairs were to be removed, a chimney altered, a fire-place built, windows and doors shifted, is merely mentioned to show that one should not be discouraged or deterred by apparently serious obstacles. That we planned as we did, and then went on to carry out the plan, is set down merely to point out that any one could and should look upon reasonably desired results as reasonably attainable if gone after with confidence. *Audace, audace, toujours audace!*

The lower floor of the wing, cut up as it was into two rooms, with a hall between, from which one stair led up and another down, made a situation without possible good treatment or good use as it stood.

The partitions were torn down, that being a very brief task. It was good fortune that the beams in the ceiling ran crosswise of the rooms. Had they run the long way and rested on the partitions, support would have been necessary when the partitions were removed. Probably a heavy and visible square timber would have been set across, to carry the weight, and in that case the entire ceiling would have been continued similarly to give a complete timbered effect; but all the timbers excepting the supporting one would have been hollow boxes so as to give the desired appearance without adding great weight. The obvious expedient of putting in supporting pillars we would not have adopted, for they would have broken the lines of the room.

The removal of the two staircases was another

thing that gave big-seeming results from small work, and then came the necessary plastering and flooring repairs to fill the spaces. And we realized that, if there had to be a repair in hard-wood flooring, it was well that it came, as did this, in the center of the room, because a rug would be sure to be there when it came to the furnishing.

Well, we had now attained to unattractive chaos; apparent chaos and certain unattract-iveness. We had a bare, unsightly, hopeless, disconsolate room, thirty feet by fifteen, by eight feet nine in height, with fragments of three kinds of wall-paper staring from the sides and with ceiling and floor both prom-inently patched.

At the front end of the room was a meager-looking door and an inadequate window, opening upon the splendid view. The opposite end showed only a smudged stove-pipe hole up near the ceiling to suggest the fireplace and hearth of our hopes.

It was now a room with six doors and four windows, and the ridiculous redundance of doors was at once reduced by taking out four useless ones and lathing and plastering flush with the wall where they had stood. In a multitude of doorways is unwisdom.

That the floor level of the wing was a little higher than that of the rest of the house, thus making the library reachable by a rise of a couple of steps, was a distinct aid in giving to the room an air of seclusion and retirement. Had this difference in floor level been between other rooms—say, between bedroom and hall, or kitchen and dining-room—it would have been a defect, a drawback, a fault; but here, taking advantage of it to set apart the library, it was a pleasurable benefit.

The door of approach, one of the two doors that were allowed to remain, opened from the parlor; the other, opposite, upon a little outside portico. But this portico door was needlessly insignificant and, therefore, was replaced by an old "Dutch" door that we had obtained from an ancient house. The door was heavy and broad, and swung massively in its disjoined halves. So heavy a door deserved a heavy knocker, and the great, black, iron one that we put upon it had been secured years before, from the door of an old house that was in the very process of demolition in the very shadow of Westminster Abbey. It was spied in an opportune moment, and the offer of a shilling for it saved it from being tossed away as rubbish.

In the portico we set an old time-eaten chest of oak, piratically iron-banded and strong, and contrived to pay the double duty of wood-box and bench.

Long iron strap hinges, and a ponderous-keyed lock half-way between knapsack and cartridge-box in size, added to the charm of the door, but it needed a row of iron-studded bolt heads to accentuate its effect. But studding bolts were hard to find; and, even if found, would have been difficult of manipulation. So, bolt-headed upholsterer's tacks, three-quarters of an inch across the top, were obtained, and driven in, four inches apart, in a marginal row. Iron tacks of required shape could not be found; only tacks of dull brass; but a touch of black metal paint, the kind so admirable for iron fireplace fittings, transformed the big brass tacks into studding sufficiently stern.

It is admirable for a library to have small window-panes as an aid in maintaining the sense of privacy, rather than great panes of glass

that seem to bring in the distractions of all outdoors. But small panes do not mean small or
insufficient windows. That fascinating library
of Romola's father, long and dusky and dim
and small-windowed, would have been the better
for plenty of light, and the old scholar's eyes
would not have failed him so soon.

Of small panes nothing carries more attractiveness than the diamond shape, and for the
window end of our own library we knew that the
diamond panes were what we wanted. And
Fortune was very good to us. In the loft of the
barn were eight diamond-pane windows, thrown
away and forgotten, and there was crescendoed
joy when, one by one, they were unearthed from
scrappy hay in dusky corners. They had never
been used in this house. No one knew how
long they had lain in the barn, or who had
gathered them, or where, and they thus strangely
came to us from unknown hands out of the
shadowy past.

They were sadly shabby and shattered, but a
mechanic of the old school was found, an old
German, careful, patient, skillful, painstaking,
and his eyes lighted with pleasure as the work
was shown to him.

ADVENTURES IN HOME-MAKING

Two were hopelessly broken; but that was no disadvantage, because the wall had room for only six!

He spread the latticed sash out and worked over them with a sort of eager and patient devotion, and, giving the two worst broken to the needs of the others, he transferred panes of glass and tiny criss-cross bars till six were complete. There were fifty-eight pieces of glass in each sash, in panes and marginal half-panes— three hundred and forty-eight for the six—and it is a literal fact that the two windows too far gone for repair yielded precisely enough glass to repair the others!—precisely enough, to a pane, with no piece to buy and none to spare. They furnished, too, sufficient cross-pieces to mend the other sash. That everything comes to the man who waits is perniciously untrue, but that everything comes to the man who looks and hopes may be set down as an axiom.

The group of windows, each of them of just the proper height and slenderness, occupied a space ten feet four by five feet six, giving opportunity for a window-seat below and a shelf above, with enough wall at either end for a narrow bookcase. And this was not that we were

[62]

THE DIAMOND-PANE WINDOWS OF THE LIBRARY

unusually fortunate, for every one may confidently hope for friendly coincidences if he will but take his desires fairly in hand and venture forth to satisfy them.

The windows, on the inside, were not set in the ordinary way, with each one recessed in a separate frame, but received an added touch of effectiveness by being flush with the inside wall, without sills, and without a raised break between the sash, the division pieces also being flush. This could not be done with raisable windows, but only with such as are fixed or casemented.

The two center sash were set as swinging casements, with the others fixed; and the inside flushness gave broad sills to the outside and dignified deep mullions.

The casements swing inward, for it is easier thus to close them hastily in case of storm, and they also permit of permanent fly-screens in summer-time. Practical considerations these; and it was another practical consideration which led to the anxious remark, from a colored woman who was cleaning the floor and looking doubtfully askance at the windows:

"I do suttunly hope, suh, that you has dem

li'l panes loose so's dey kin be took out an' put undah de pump to wash 'em!''

A long window-seat came naturally. For a room like this one thinks at once of such a usable window-seat as that in the studio of Trilby's friends, which "spread itself in width and length and delightful thickness." Many window-seats are too narrow for sitting and too short for lying and too impracticable for anything else.

The seat was given just the length of the windowed space, and a comfortable two feet of width. A six-foot stretch in the center is covered with a woven-wire spring, but each end is boarded over. A three-inch-thick mattress upholstered in heavy woolen cloth is over the entire length, and in measuring for cloth for this or a similar purpose the upholsterer's rule should be remembered, that one-seventh must be added to each dimension for tufting, for otherwise there will be provoking scantiness.

On this long window-bench eight people may coincidently sit, three may coincidently lounge, and one alone may lie or lounge or sit, and read in the best of lights or look off at a long-distance view.

Above the diamond-pane windows was placed a broad shelf running from side to side of the room. Now, such a shelf would be the reverse of desirable; it would be a distinct mistake; if there were not befitting things to place upon it. If it were to remain empty it would be a blemish; and, if covered with a medley of knick-knacks, an even worse blemish. We put up this shelf to hold a collection of old pewter: tankards, beakers, a bowl for spices, a lamp, all backed by a line of plates and platters. The great advantage of old pewter as a decoration is its soft glow of color and its fine simplicity; while its close connection with the daily and intimate life of the past gives it a touch of peculiar fascination. And that the pieces have been gradually gathered, in New York, Massachusetts, Pennsylvania, in odd corners of Normandy, in Reuss, in Padua, in the Dolomites, adds pleasurable value.

The shelf needed braces to hold it up, but braces in sight would be a marked blemish, especially as the usual braces have an ugly hypothenused bar, and so an effort was made to use braces invisibly.

From a blacksmith three angles of iron,

three-quarters of an inch wide and eight inches in each arm, were bought for eight cents each, pierced with screw holes. One bar of each of these was fastened to the shelf; but to the top side, not the bottom. Then two of the vertical ends were set downward and screwed tight, out of sight behind the window-casing, and the third was set above the shelf and was afterward covered with plaster and wall-paper.

Now what should the bookshelves themselves be? This was an important matter indeed.

It usually looks best and costs least to have shelves made for the particular room and built into it. It is the American custom of frequent changes of home that makes people hesitate to build in bookcases which can not be carried away with them; though, oddly enough, the same people will not hesitate to lay hard-wood floors and build porches without considering that they, likewise, can not be moved.

This new room of ours had thirty-five and a half feet to be devoted to shelving, this taking in all of the wall-length except the chimney-corners, and seeming to put shelves all around the the room. Of course, we hoped to have cases

of good design; and they were, at the same
time, to be fittingly inconspicuous, as cases
are primarily but a support and a background
for the most important feature of a library,
the books.

We decided to have low-set cases, because
they hold and display the books while, at the
same time, they do so without so encroaching
on the wall surface as to prevent the free and
effective hanging of pictures.

The plan was presented to the contracting
carpenter, with all the various measurements
and with sketches showing the desired design of
the proposed pilasters and the simple cornicing.
There were to be five separate cases, besides
small return cases filling the short space between
the diamond-paned windows and the side wall
and giving a marked sense of completeness to
the plan. Most of the cases were to be single
sections, between door and window or window
and window, but one was to cover a long
stretch in which several divisions would be
needed.

For material, birch was decided upon, for it
could easily be stained mahogany color. Mahogany itself would have been much more

expensive and, being a harder wood, would also have involved considerable more cost in the labor of making it.

We might have planned to paint the cases white, instead of finishing them as mahogany, for white bookcases have a very great charm; only it is the kind of charm that goes most fittingly with a woman's boudoir type of room. Or, we might have decided upon fumed oak, which is used with great success in many modern libraries; only fumed oak seems to demand a craftsman or old English setting, nor would it be in harmony with our old mahogany furniture. So the birch, mahogany stained, was chosen.

The height of the cases was to be four and a half feet, thus making it convenient to open a book upon the top, and permitting the hanging of pictures at the ideal height of the eye-line.

There were to be four shelves, at graduated heights, in each case, and the lowest was to be six inches above the floor to make it more convenient to reach the books and read the titles on that lowest shelf, and at the same time to establish for the books a protection from feet and brooms. It is customary, for some unexplainable reason, to have a corrugated and projecting molding below the bottom shelf of low bookcases, whereas there ought to be a plain and vertical board there, set back a trifle from the shelf line to minimize toe-stub marks.

At intervals there were to be plain pilasters to mask the narrow edges of shelf-supporting boards which, unmasked, would give an effect of rude boxiness. These pilasters were to be four inches wide at the floor, diminishing to three at the top, and were to have narrow capitals of small molding, which itself was to be the same height with a line of similar molding running under the length of the flat top of the cases. The design for this molding was taken from the simple molding of the mantel-piece already chosen for this room.

Pilasters were equally needful at the ends as at these intervals of support, and with the end pilasters a puzzling problem presented itself, for the outside edges needed to be vertical. With much doubt, for we feared some queer result, the carpenter was told to run the outside edge of each terminal pilaster straight up and down, and the inside edge on a tapering line. And this turned out so well that not only is the needful terminal straightness preserved, but the eye fails to detect that there is any variation in the taperings.

The shelves were to be ten inches wide and the top twelve inches. We had been warned against any greater length of unsupported shelf than thirty-six inches, but, thinking that a repetition of such short sections would not look well, involving, as it would, so many pilastered breaks, we risked fifty-four inches for several of them; and, the wood being well-seasoned and good, have had no reason to repent it, while, at the same time, finding the long, unbroken rows of books far more attractive than shorter ones would be. And if, at any time, a shelf should warp, it will simply need to be turned over, to straighten it.

There was to be no woodwork and, of course, no wall-paper, behind the books, and the wall there was merely to be painted an inconspicuous reddish brown.

For the cases and shelves the bid was only sixty-one dollars, all fitted in place; this last being an important point, especially in building-in cases in an old house, as a great deal of what carpenters call "scribing" would be necessary—that is, cutting to fit to a somewhat irregular wall surface.

The bid was accepted, but there was, after all, a good deal of risk, for there was no certainty as to what the mill, with which the carpenter placed the order, would bring forth. But the results were in every particular admirable, each detail being seen to just as we hoped for.

And there was one detail that came with humorous unexpectedness. As there would be quite a difference in cost between fixed shelves and shelves arranged to adjust in height at will, the adjustable seemed really an unnecessary expense, in view of the many other things to be done about the new home, and so the carpenter was given definite measures for the spacing, and no mention at all was made of making the shelves movable.

But when they came they were found to be adjustable, after all! And the carpenter said, apologetically: "I got some of those measures mixed, and I was afraid they'd be wrong, and so I just had all the shelves made for adjustable heights. You like them just as well, don't you?" he added, a little anxiously.

We did.

CHAPTER IV

A FIREPLACE AND A SECRET STAIR

OUR adventures in home-making taught us many things; among them, the fact that it is easy to put in a fireplace. Ordinarily a man considers that he has a house with fireplaces or a house without fireplaces; it is looked upon as a fixed condition; whereas, as a matter of fact, it need not at all be a fixed condition, but is subject to one's own judgment and desires. Naturally there are differences as to the ease with which fireplaces may be put in where they do not already exist, but it will usually be found that with a little adaptability the putting in can be readily arranged.

Among the curious and well-nigh incomprehensible things of the past century was the passing of the fireplace in favor of the air-tight stove and the furnace. It used to be, of necessity, that every house had its fireplaces. Then they were swiftly discarded, with none so poor to do them reverence. But gradually they have been coming into their delightful own again, with improvements that come from a better knowledge of chimneys and of the conservation of heat. The mere fact that stoves and furnaces and hot-water apparatus are quite capable of heating a house without the aid from an open fire is no good reason why the open fire should be entirely given up; for with it one gives up so much of the keenest pleasure of living. It would be foolish not to make use of the admirable modern improvements in heating, but it would be quite as foolish not to use open fires as auxiliaries, for their charm and healthfulness.

To sit beside an open fire is to yield to an instinct as old as all life and all nature. The very animals have it. Your dog is ecstatically happy, lying outstretched at your feet, with his eyes blinking at the blaze. And as to cats, was it not Southey who remarked that the fireside is the cat's Eden? All races of mankind, savage and civilized, have yielded to the fascination of the open blaze. Did you ever see, in a room where there was a blaze in the fireplace, a single person's eyes turned away from it except temporarily? Did you ever see campers, lying down at night about a fire, turn their backs to it?

No wonder that the ancient belief had it that the first fire came down from Heaven. No wonder the ancient Romans incorporated the hearthstone blaze in the worship of their Lares. No wonder that the Americans have swiftly returned to the love of open fires, after the brief period during which only the supposedly "old-fashioned" clung to them. A flickering fireplace is a joy.

This house which was to be our home was to rely for most of its heat upon a big and capable furnace, but we wished fireplaces as well. The house was not without them, but there was none in the big long room that had been evolved from small ones and which was to be the library; and it was precisely a room in which a fireplace was needed. Fortunately, as is usually the case when problems are approached in the expectation of success, the difficulties were far from insurmountable.

Although there was no fireplace, there was a chimney at the end of the room where the fireplace was needed, facing the diamond-paned windows, and it had a chimney-breast projecting the dignified distance of two feet eight, thus giving space sufficient for a fireplace. Far up on the wall there was a pipe-hole, but it needed only to be filled in and plastered over. By good fortune, the chimney had been continued to the floor, with supporting columns of brick running down into the cellar, making it easily possible to go ahead with the fireplace without preliminary chimney building.

By some freakish chance, the chimney-breast was not in the middle of the wall; nor was it far enough to one side to make it a corner fireplace had we wished for this. It was merely and tantalizingly off center, and so the thing to do was to have it widened, with eighteen inches of lath and plaster front, to put it in the middle. This was done; and when the work was finally completed, and the chimney-breast papered, there was absolutely nothing to indicate that there had ever been off-centering.

This widening of the chimney-breast left a space behind the new lath and plaster, and this space was utilized as a chimney closet, with door opening to the side.

The fireplace, of course, was opened in the

very center of the new chimney-breast; it was a simple bit of mason work, easily done, and there was no trouble in keeping it in connection with the flue, although that was now at one side.

When a chimney is in existence before the fireplace is planned, the size of the fireplace opening can not be a matter of taste or fancy, for between chimney-flue and fireplace opening there must be a recognized proportion if the chimney is to draw properly. It is the frequent neglect of this proportion in building or adapting which gives rise to the popular belief that smoky fires will happen with even the best-regulated fireplaces.

The sectional area of the opening of the fireplace should be ten times the sectional area of the flue. Our flue was nine by twelve, an area of one hundred and eight square inches. The fireplace opening, therefore, needed to be one thousand and eighty, and this area was best attained by making the opening thirty-six inches wide and thirty inches high—which again was good fortune, for it was a size that was entirely satisfactory, in looks, for the place.

We took two of our old-fashioned mantel-pieces—we had several that we had gathered in at points several hundred miles apart—and held them up at the fireplace to see which looked best, like draping a bit of dress goods or a suit on a figure, and decided upon the one which went best with the size of the chimney-breast and the thirty-six by thirty. With its simple and admirable lines it took its place with as natural an air as if it had been made for that particular spot.

The mantel had but one defect—a vertical crack across the center panel, beneath the shelf. Paint could not hide it, nor inserted splinters cure its contrariety. After each effort (to anticipate a little) it gaped newly with the heat of a few fires, and it again did so after the painter filled it with "composition" and after the carpenter, spurred to renewed effort, planed it close with his tiniest plane. But at length the solution of the problem came. Decorator's canvas was fitted and glued into the panel and painted the color of the mantel-piece, and the trouble was over.

A throttle (a chimney damper) was built in, so that at any time the flue could be entirely shut, the ability to close a fireplace flue being not infrequently a convenience: in the coldest

[77]

weather to retain in the room the heat of the furnace, in damp weather to keep soot-scale from falling into the room, and in summer to keep out chimney-swifts.

Red brick tile, unglazed, and four inches square, an admirable imitation of Moravian tile anciently made in this vicinity, were bought at a pottery but a dozen miles distant, where they are made in the old-fashioned way: roughly worked by hand, and punched from the clay as a housewife cuts a cooky from dough. These fitted the space on the vertical front, between the fire-place opening and the mantel-piece, six inches at each side and eight inches above— and they were also laid as a hearth, twenty inches broad.

The hearth tile were laid upon a fire-proof bed of thick concrete. All the tile were set in place in pure lime, mixed with a little lampblack; and thus there are lines of black plaster between each of the tiles, a simple way to gain an effect- ive result. The lime oozed up a little between the tile, as they were tapped into place, but it would have been a mistake to rub this off at once; instead, it was allowed to stand for twenty-four hours, till quite hardened, when it was crumbled off clean, and the line smoothed with a steel point.

The work of setting the tile was not done by an experienced tile-setter; that would have involved getting a man out from the city, with delay and expense. The tile were bought and sent to the house, and a local mason, who was building the laundry chimney, was given the work of setting them. He built a frame, to fill the fireplace opening, and this supported the weight of the upper rows until they "set." The tile, both on the hearth and on the face, were guided in straight rows, in the laying, by means of a string, that the man advanced as he worked. It was so simply and easily done, and was so fascinating in its progress, that when, later, a hearth was to be laid in another room, it was merely taken as an easy and successful bit of home work.

Unglazed tile of this sort, and also ordinary unpainted brick, gain in increasing softness of color, increasing mellowness of tone, with time and use and rubbings with linseed oil. Following the advice of the tile makers, to hasten the mellowing process, each of the library tile was laid for half an hour in boiling linseed oil, not deep enough for complete immersion, but just deep enough to treat the side that was to face outward; had the other side been wetted with the oil it would have spoiled the tile for adhesion. Well, the desired color was gained—but all too soon it was lost, and in an annoyingly amusing way. For at the first cleaning of the completed room, a time-saving scrubber took off all the mellowness with lye used in cleaning the floor, whereby all the linseed labor was lost, and it took months of oil-rubbing and use to secure the proper coloring again. And, anyhow, on the whole this Dark-Ages process of boiling in oil proved altogether too much of a task for its results, and with our next hearth laying we did without it and found our reward in trusting to time and smoke and rubbing.

There was choice of brass andirons ready to put in the fireplace, for we had been gathering old things for years that now would fit admirably into this house that throughout we were to keep old-fashioned. The pair of andirons selected were beautiful rights and lefts from an old house in the Western Reserve, which brought with them the very atmosphere of the past.

The fireback, the reredos, came still farther.

THE FIREPLACE END OF THE LIBRARY, AS FINISHED

A FIREPLACE AND A SECRET STAIR

We had discovered it, six years before, in the house of a cobbler in the village of St. Cloud. He had it from his father, who had taken it from the Chateau of St. Cloud at the time of its burning and looting during the siege of Paris. We did not take it when we first came across it, not then having a home of our own to build it into, and it being too heavy (eighty pounds) to carry about just for the pleasure of possessing it. But now was the time to get it. One of us happened to be in Paris, took a run out to St. Cloud before sailing, found the cobbler and the reredos and the same price—only ten francs—and it was brought over on the steamer, and is in place, a proud possession, with its old royal arms, and its fine motto, of the time of Louis the Fourteenth, still decipherable: *Seul Contre Tous.*

If this motto had not come to us it is probable that we should not have had one in the library, for it is a difficult thing to put a motto there which avoids being trite or pretentious. Yet the custom of putting a motto in the library has certainly the approval of the centuries, and the motto of the very oldest library of which history tells, that of an Egyptian king, was: "A Storehouse of Medicine for the Mind."

Upon the mantel there was to be nothing but two brass candlesticks, and above the mantel a single picture, it being of vital importance to avoid a cluttered appearance about a fireplace, and to exercise discriminative reserve.

A tall picture, high enough to reach to the cornice line, was decided upon, and it was to be so fastened, flat against the wall, as to seem part of the permanent decoration of the room.

The picture was one of the admirable modern German school, representing a highly-pictorial line of knights and lances above a shadowy red-roofed town. It is a dark, strong picture, strong in treatment and in color effects, and on strong paper. And the question came, why put glass over it?—why not leave it as if it were a painting?

And so, rolled in its paper cylinder, it was taken in to an artists' material shop, and a meager, bent-over German came forward, a man of aspect crusty and crabbed and cross, but whose real nature proved to be divertingly different from this outward crust.

"I should like to look at a stretcher, a canvas, to mount this picture on."

A FIREPLACE AND A SECRET STAIR

The answer came snappishly: "No canvas used now—all cotton!"

"All right, cotton."

"But—but—paste that color-print on!" he spluttered irascibly. "Nobody but an expert can do that!"

"Well, I should like it done."

"*You* can't do it!" He glared, but instead of insisting on impossibility became suddenly helpful. "My man is an expert, and while he's making the stretcher he'll just paste it on. It'll take him only a few minutes."

"And I want some varnish for it."

"Varnish!" he exclaimed explosively. "That can't be varnished! It needs mastic!"

"Very well—I meant mastic varnish."

"Mastic's the thing! But do you know how hard it is to put mastic on without spoiling the picture?" he demanded. "It must have a thin coat of thin rice-flour paste first!"

"Well, paste, then." To know this man was beginning to be a liberal education.

"Hum!" He hesitated, and looked for a moment mollified. "My man will put it on."

"And the mastic——"

"The mastic! You can't put that on right! You'd put too much on and it would run!"

"But your man ——"

"He can't do it! I can't do it myself! You can't do it!"

"Well, there's a painter working at the house, who understands mahogany finishing and that sort of thing. I'll get him to do it with a camel's-hair brush."

"Huh!" He sold the mastic, but with continuous pessimism as to results. The stretcher was perfectly made and treated, and the total charge for this and the mastic was only a dollar and thirty cents. At home the painter applied the mastic with quick, light strokes, and the picture, protected by the mastic from the air, and with all the effect of a painting, was ready for a frame.

The frame was to be plain black, and in the house was the very thing—but not in the shape of a frame!

In the dining-room, some simple pine molding of good design, four inches wide without too many curves, was being used. And it was precisely the proper design for the frame, and cost but four cents a foot.

A FIREPLACE AND A SECRET STAIR

A carpenter, working at the house, cut the molding, and mitered the corners and fitted them together—a hard thing to do, although it seems theoretically so simple. In cutting and mitering, the wood was not held flat, but was cut on a bevel so as to make the picture stand out in a relief of two inches. It was fastened vertically in place with nails, and the heads were countersunk and puttied over. The frame, with two coats of dead black paint, was as satisfactory in appearance as if it were a frame expensively obtained of a dealer.

From the first, we had every reason to felicitate ourselves that we were to live in the house while the work was going one, for day by day we realized that only thus was it possible to give to the house the care and thought and oversight so peculiarly demanded by alteration work of this character, and that could not have been given by coming from a distance, no matter how frequently, to watch progress. It was clear how imperatively needful was personal presence in the house, even though the smell of the plaster was over it all and the sound of the hammer was heard in the land. Yet it was certainly something of an experience to live for weeks with a good share of the household belongings in boxes, including the books that were waiting for the completion of the library.

The tiles of the fireplace were a rich red-brown, to match the mahogany color of the book-cases. The window-seat was real mahogany, its front being made of five panels from an old mahogany door, and the broad Dutch door was put into the color of mahogany. The window-frames and the mantel-piece were cream white. At the diamond-paned windows there were to be no curtains, but for the other windows were chosen silk-tissue curtains of a fine golden brown, which, in a pattern of small diamonds, are precisely the thing for the room. It may be worth while to mention that these curtains, so fortuitously bediamonded, were picked up, by a happy chance, for one-sixth their usual price.

And now the question came, what color should the wall be? If tradition were to be followed it would be a dark or even somber color. A green would have been really fine, but, personally, we happened to desire something else; and, after all, one's personal fancy should always have weight if within the limits of good taste. Woodwork in French gray, with wall-paper the same except for being of a shade a trifle darker, makes an attractive but austere room a little cold. Repose and warmth and quietness of effect are imperatively requisite in a library; and with the dark cases and white windows and mantel it seemed as if a shade of tobacco brown would be best, and so a half dozen long sample pieces were held up against the wall in turn. But none of them seemed just right.

At length we decided to take a risk. We chose a yellow—King's yellow, or, as it might more irreverently be termed, pumpkin yellow— not to brighten the room, but to warm it, while at the same time giving a really beautiful color. Absolutely patternless, it was color alone, and, to go with it, the ceiling was given a paper of cream-white, like that of the mantel.

But in one respect, an important respect, it was not a success. At the fireplace end of the room, on either side of the chimney-breast, there was a glow of the yellow from ceiling to floor, and that the yellow was a good yellow could not hide the fact that there was too much of it.

How was the fault to be remedied? This question presented itself insistently.

Would it be well to paper the lower half of the room there with the tobacco brown? Not bad, yet not quite the right solution. Another idea, dismissed as soon as entertained, was to put some sort of tapestry there, some hanging or something in Eastern coloring perhaps; but we felt strongly opposed to the kind of fussy cozy-corner which such things inevitably make. Then would it be well to give up the yellow entirely and paper over it, in some other color, for the entire room? This last plan was seriously considered.

The problem was mulled over for days, and was at length solved by panels that were at least unique in the making.

Molding, identical with that used as the top line of each bookcase, was fastened against the wall on the level of the bookcase tops, on both sides of the chimney-breast.

Then a light little molding, in tall, slim rectangles, was nailed with fine finishing nails against the papered wall between the first molding and the baseboard, leaving a three-inch space above and below, with six inches between panels. This was enthusiastically done, with a saw and a miter-box and a foot-rule, the evening that the idea came, after the carpenter had gone home; and there were rectangles of molding placed even underneath the windows to give completely an air of verisimilitude.

This simple work was all that was needed! —all except painting. For the lower half of that part of the room—molding and baseboard and wall-paper—was merely painted cream-white, and no one looking at it has doubted but that all that surface is paneled in wood.

A highly-important single factor was that the wall-paper had, by good luck, a smooth-textured, fibery surface that took paint like a board. Even then, had the paint line ended with the wall-paper against wall-paper, an oily stain would have continued ahead, but this was averted by ending with the baseboard on the bottom, and with the line of molding, bookcase high, at the top. And, too, the slight projection of this line of molding makes an apparent throwing out of the entire painted space below it to a different plane from that of the wall-paper above, and this aids materially in maintaining the effect. And it was all so easily done! Fourteen mitered rectangles on a papered surface gave us fourteen sunken panels and a wainscoted wall. And, practical consideration, it cost so little!—for the sticks used as molding, ninety-six cents, and nothing else but the painting. The entire wall was now right, retaining the fine warm yellow coloring, but with no longer too much of it and with all in the upper part of the room.

The long, unbroken wall spaces for the bookcases and the paneling were not in the room originally; were not there when the room had been developed from the little ones and partitions and stairs had been eliminated. On the contrary, the walls were broken with what seemed numberless doors; one to the front, which was removed for the diamond-paned windows, one to the side portico, which was replaced by the broad Dutch door, one, a quite necessary one, into the parlor—but three others utterly unnecessary, utterly superfluous; useless doors that only disturbed the line of the walls. These three had to be taken out, and the spaces where they had stood had to be lathed and plastered and wall-papered to leave not the slightest sign that they had ever existed.

In conclusion, came the pleasant details of furnishing. Rugs for the floor? Surely noth-

ing can be better. Books to fill the shelves—
and arranged not only by subjects, but with
heedful regard for evenness, regularity, and
heights, for neglect of this gives a general air of
untidiness. Pictures for the walls; and hung
on the eye-line, almost directly upon the top of
the bookcases or paneling, but yet with avoidance
of actually resting there.

It is so easy to put things on the top of low
bookcases that the tendency to clutter must be
sternly resisted. But resist the devil of cluttery-
ness and he will flee from thee. On these bookcase tops are a very few things, and only such
as harmonize in color and character with the
general character and color of the room: a tall
jar of early American pottery, an old silver
candlestick, an apostle bowl, a brass kettle, of
delectable shape, picked up in Schnee-Eifel Land,
an old French clock, with case of mahogany
overlaid with curious arabesques of dull brass.
Thus the long rows of bookcase tops were left
practically bare.

The sense of space and freedom in a room is
very desirable, and yet even a large room can be
so broken and belittled by the placing of the
furniture as to give it essentially no advantage

over a smaller one. Therefore this room was
to have an unbroken stretch of floor from hearth
to window-seat; the furniture that gained ad-
mission was to be so arranged as not to break
the central stretch but only to border it, and
was not put in merely because we had it but
because it would be suitable and useful in a quiet
library; an old slant-top desk, rich in pigeon-
holes and drawers; an ancient fireside chair,
an ideal reading chair, from the fascinating
Eastern Shore, where it was discovered cast
away in a chicken-house; a little table, with
raised rim, that had come to us through the
friendship of an octogenarian who had a definite
history of it as far back as the time of his great-
grandmother; a chair that came ancestrally
from over seas; a few other chairs congruent and
comfortable; a chest.

Now, it should not be understood that every
particle of the work in the library was finished
before any other work elsewhere was even begun. The library was the first begun; it was
the first finished; until finished, it had the main
part of our attention; but always there was more
or less to do elsewhere; always there were other
things, outdoors and in, to push on coincidently.

A FIREPLACE AND A SECRET STAIR

From the first, when taking down the impossible partition and stairs in the middle of the room, we knew that an extra bedroom and a sewing-room, directly above the library, would not be accessible except through another sleeping-room, if some new way of reaching them from below could not be contrived. But there had been no hesitation about destroying the stairs, for unless they were cleared away the library would be an impossibility, and it was assuredly well worth while to make some sacrifice, if needful, for such a result as this long room.

One day, through the suggestion of a friend, the solution came: "Can't you put in a secret stair beside the fireplace?"

Now, there is perennial delight in a secret stair—and here was the chance to have a stair both secret and at the same time highly practical. At once there came thoughts of many secret stairs of history and fiction: of the one in Henry Esmond, set in a window-sill; of the one pictured by Balzac, entered by pushing aside the very back of a fireplace, and therefore so often so delightfully unusable; of the stairs in the walls at Blois.

And so the thought of a secret stair grew upon us. It seemed just the thing to round out what had been done in the room, and always with the satisfactory feeling that, in following the leading of romance, we were making a very usable and necessary addition to the house.

Measurements were taken to test the practical feasibility, and plans were definitely made, and then the carpenter was called in and the case presented to him.

"You can cut through this paneling beside the fireplace into the little room behind," he was told. "Keep the baseboard in place; it can always be stepped over. The entrance way through the paneling, and the spring to push to open it, must not show. Begin the stair in the storeroom, boarding it in there so as to have no entrance from that side. Run the stair up within the chimney-breast, utilizing the upper part of the closet space beside the chimney, and take advantage of the fact that the flue begins to angle over toward one side at the height of six and a half feet. There must be nothing to give a hint that the chimney conceals a stair. And now, is it feasible, and if so how much will it cost?"

THE FIREBACK FROM ST. CLOUD (See page 81.)

THE PANEL ENTRANCE OF THE SECRET STAIR

A FIREPLACE AND A SECRET STAIR

The carpenter, happily accustomed by other work here to look upon the unusual as usual, came and saw and was conquered. "Nothing easier," he said laconically. "It will be steep and narrow, but there is headway enough. I guess that's how a secret stair ought to be, though I never built one before. There will be a little new wood to get, besides what I see left here from the other jobs, and the labor will be, I think, not over twelve dollars. It will certainly not be over eighteen."

And thereupon, thus simply, the secret stairs were made.

CHAPTER V

DEALING WITH AN OLD PARLOR

A WHIMSICAL experience in connection with the very beginning of our experiences here might well be called The Adventure of the Blue Tiling; and it was not only whimsical but highly to our advantage as well. And the basis of it was the tiles' very ugliness!

For there may be merit in ugliness; there may be very real merit in impossible shades of glaring and glittering blue; and in this case the merit, which was as unexpected as it was desirable, was the lessening of the purchase price of the house!

This eye-piercing blue was set aggressively around the fireplace in the parlor. It was noticeable even in the match-light initial inspection, and was positively startling when one of the solid shutters was swung open and the sunlight struck full upon it. These tiles not only killed that room but exercised a baleful influence throughout the entire house. They had been put in place in the Dark Ages of taste, something over a quarter of a century ago, and, not content with one-shade ugliness, there were varieties three—the background color, and upon it, on each tile, a blue-faced woman with a still brighter blue of Medusa-like hair. The owner from whom we bought had never lived in the house and was not responsible for either its good or its evil. He realized the ugliness of the tile, and was so vexed at having to offer for sale a house thus decorated that he actually set the price lower than he otherwise would have done.

Naturally, one of the first things to be done after getting the house was to pry off those offending tiles. It needed but a few minutes' work with a chisel, a little smoothing, and a coat of white kalsomine where the tiles had stood, and presto! they had vanished! Then, with the mantel-piece painted white, the effect was highly satisfactory, for the mantel-piece, as old as this central part of the house, and, therefore pre-Revolutionary, is one of real beauty.

As a matter of fact, the kalsomining of the plaster was intended to be only temporary, and

7

as soon as possible tiles of proper color were to be put in place of the blue tiles removed, but the plain white surface proved to be so suitable and good-looking that to change it would have been a mistake.

The old hearth was of half a dozen quarreling shades of black and red, and it was chopped out and replaced with buff-colored tile of the same Moravian make that we had put in the library—tiles that are of a slight but delightful irregularity in shape and surface, to avoid machine-like effect, and which have all the charm of appearance of the hand-made.

It was a positive joy to restore and outfit this room. Built in the long ago, part of the old portion of the house, its four windows were deeply recessed, with window-sills full fifteen inches in depth and with fine reedings cut out by the old-time builder on the recessed panels above the sills.

This room was ideally and uniquely planned in that it had a pair of windows at both front and back, the front ones opening southward, looking out toward the principal view, the others toward the northward, looking out upon a brick-paved porch, a low-walled formal garden, and an avenue of trees; and this uniqueness of construction gave to the room great charm.

From the first, there were joyous possibilities here, as there are in almost every room made heedfully by the builders of over a century ago, for there was in those years, in building, a sort of instinct for proportion and fitness and form. Nor were the builders of that time hampered, and their taste and instincts crushed, by the necessity, that usually faces the worker of to-day, of using ready-made, mill-made products.

A new floor was imperative, for the old floor, of broad pine boards, had always been too rough for polishing, had become somewhat punky from age, and was battered and worn. Set between hall and wing, and occupying the full depth of the center of the house, the room had paid the penalty of having to be often walked across. And this points out the radical difference between a house with rooms grouped about a center and a house with rooms spread across a long front; the grouped house offering little of that sense of isolated seclusion so delightful in a home, and the long house giving great seclusion in some rooms and of necessity making a passageway of others.

Had it been possible, the floor would have been left unchanged, for in doing over an old house it is the reverse of desirable to do away with things which give an air and atmosphere of the past and try to make the house look as if it were built yesterday. A little roughness, a little irregularity, are more delightful than when art is too precise in every part, for an important part of the charm of an old house is its very appearance and suggestion of age, its summoning up of remembrance of things past.

The new floor was, of course, to be of hardwood, for few things so add to the appearance of a house as a hardwood floor. It adds also to the healthfulness, because it does not harbor dirt. But like all really fine things a hardwood floor needs care. Indeed, the old-time hymnmaker almost sang, "The perils that afflict hard floors in number many be."

Yes, he who puts in a hardwood floor is laying up trouble for himself; for he becomes for a time the most sensitive of beings, and to him there is no blacker crime in the calendar than to mar his floor with heel-plates or to scratch it by the careless shove-back of a chair. And there are dangers from umbrellas and wet rubbers and

THE PRESENT APPEARANCE OF THE OLDEST ROOM IN THE HOUSE

from the toes of your own pet dog, besides the dangers which come from cleaning-day and the moving of furniture and the patter of many feet.

The cost of a hardwood floor is no longer prohibitive. The great shops of the larger cities will lay a floor at a price depending on material, and will even send their men to near-by towns, or they will ship the flooring to points farther away. The bid for this room, and it was accepted, was forty-seven dollars for putting down and completely finishing the floor, in quarter-sawed, white oak; the room being seventeen and a half feet by sixteen and a half.

When one comes to appreciate a polished hardwood floor nothing else approaches it in its sense of satisfaction. But in this matter, as in everything else, there are viewpoints various. We remember a lady who particularly loved to visit the Louvre on account of its polished floors, because, as she naïvely said, it gave her little girl such sliding places.

White oak was chosen because, of all hard-woods in America, it is best for flooring. It needs a filler, but has a firm and even grain and takes a beautiful polish. We were careful, in arranging for the floor, to see that quarter-sawed was definitely agreed to, as much beauty is added to oak by this process of cutting, it being distinguished from other woods by its "silver grain" groups of fibers which shoot out laterally from the center of the trunk toward the bark.

The term "quarter-sawing" is a mystery to many who have no way of knowing for themselves whether a piece of oak is quarter-sawed or not. And this is what the process is. Instead of slicing the log in the ordinary way it is first sawed into quarters; then each quarter has boards sawed from each of its faces as long as any remains. The result is wood with beautiful silver streaks and fleckings, showing the "silver grain" to fine advantage, in place of the shelving surfaces of plain-sawed oak—shelving surfaces that are so liable to catch and splinter.

The new flooring was only five-sixteenths of an inch thick, for it was to be laid on top of the old and thoroughly seasoned floor already in place; almost always the best way to do, under such circumstances, and at the same time much the cheapest.

In choosing the design for the floor it should be remembered that it is to have a rug. Only the East Room of the White House has a bare floor! So the middle of the floor is without pattern. The border is about as simple in effect as possible if there is to be any border at all, as it is of the same wood as the center, sixteen inches in width, and mitered at each of the four corners.

A new baseboard was at the same time put in, the old one having lost its pristine straightness and flawlessness. A poor baseboard inevitably destroys the looks of any room, and the rule should be: When in doubt, get a new one! For small expense, it gives a large result.

The mantel, in place where it had been set originally, a survival through mutation that had played havoc with other rooms, is of admirably simple and simply admirable design, and has some fine reeding, simple, charming, and restrained, that matches the reeding of the window recesses; reeding such as Sheraton was accustomed to put in his furniture. It is things like this that add to the pleasurable chances in securing an old house.

The mantel is very large for the size of the room, having a height of five feet nine inches in a room height of eight feet six inches, yet it does not seem in the slightest degree out of proportion. It is, on the contrary, convincingly right.

Proportion is one of the most subtle of all things. It can not be said that a large room requires a large mantel-piece and a small room a small mantel-piece, for the larger room may have the smaller mantel and the small room the larger mantel. There is no regular sliding scale; it is a matter of looks alone; and this applies to many things besides mantel-pieces. There can be no more striking example than is seen in the façade of the Capitol at Washington. There is splendid immensity of line and height; there are the great rows of steps sweeping upward; there is the noble overtopping dome; and then, instead of the hugely-imposing entrance which one might expect, there is a doorway scarcely larger than the entrance door of one's own house. And yet the proportion is right just because it is right.

Out of our boxed-up furniture we took for the fireplace a pair of andirons of polished brass that we obtained, once upon a time, on Blennerhasset Island, shortly after a great flood in the Ohio had deposited them there in a house that came drifting down out of the unknown.

DEALING WITH AN OLD PARLOR

This fireplace, quite the pride of our hearts in fireplaces, has the inconvenience of having the stone on which the fire burns set three inches above the hearth in front of it, making it impossible to sweep back the scattering dust and ashes inseparable from an open fire. However, this does put the fire at a more toe-toasting height, and it does follow the method of some of the great architects of the past. There is just such a raised fire hearth at Malcontenta, built by the great Palladio on the once world-famous but now forgotten Brenta.

From the first moment of possession of the house we knew that our opportunity had come for a white room; and it is one of the comforts, one of the delights, of country living, that one may realize his dreams of white without thought of soot and city stains.

White was the only proper color for this ancient wooden mantel-piece and for the windows with their paneled and reeded jambs. And white offered such a delightful and advantageous contrast with the old mahogany furniture that we were to place in the room. And this was the room that was to get the first of those mahogany doors that came from the opportunely demolished house. And we reserved for this room of white and mahogany our few paintings, all outdoor scenes, framed very simply in gold. And as the room would not have its open fire very often in use, it not being a general sitting-room and in no way dependent for warmth upon this source, there were laid in the fire-place, across the andirons, a couple of white birch logs, which can be taken out when a fire is wanted and which, meanwhile, add a really surprising degree of attractiveness. Practically all of our friends go away in search of white birch logs or to watch eagerly for the death of super-annuated white birch trees.

That white makes a room appear larger than the same-sized room treated in dark color, did not need to be considered, nor did we need to consider any scheme for adding to or diminishing the apparent height. A room, like a woman, can be so dressed as to counteract deficiencies, but the dimensions of this room were sufficiently satisfactory. And we assuredly did not need to think of theories regarding certain colors of wall-paper for a room with northern windows and certain other colors for southern!

An English paper, a pattern in ovals in felici-

"QUITE THE PRIDE OF OUR HEARTS, IN FIREPLACES."

tous Adam design, was fixed upon, in an effort to keep the room "in the epoch," as a Frenchman would say. Still, as we are not of those who are afraid to say that they have learned something since yesterday, we would now stand strongly for a patternless paper or for panels. Pictures can not be hung successfully on a patterned wall, though it is hard really to realize this, so fixed in the popular heart is wall-paper in pattern.

One thing that can not be amended with a parlor is its name; for unless the house be of sufficient importance to be a mansion, it savors of pretense to refer to a drawing-room. Most people seem to dislike both names about equally. But what, after all, is a reasonable objection to "parlor"? It has generations of usage behind it in its present sense, and Herrick has quaintly said, "Like as my parlor, so my hall and kitchen's small."

But though one may not like either of the names, there ought in every house to be a parlor or drawing-room, a room set apart for other than the every-hour use of the family, in spite of the present-day disparagement of it. Such a room stands for ideals, for not having everything on the same common plane. The household or the individual that does not have something set apart, not to be commonly used or handled, misses an important part of life.

There is always a temptation to overload in the display of treasures and to pile the Ossa of ornament on the Pelion of purchase, and although one can not quite agree with the Japanese in having practically empty rooms and bare walls, with perhaps but a single treasure showing, at least it must be admitted that the method argues a certain masterly restraint. It is better, however, to put one's things where they may be seen and enjoyed, yet without scattering them broadcast and thus ruining the room. In the parlor, trying to live up to the idea of sparing-ness, the mantel shelf is bare except for two old candlesticks of Sheffield plate, picked up in Tours, and three old Crown Derby vases, decorated in flowers and blue and gold. The rest of the room is without ornament other than the pictures and furniture, except for another silver candlestick or so, a bit of clear Venetian glass, and a large yellow amphora, of Sicilian pottery, which when bought, a mile from shore in the harbor of Palermo, contained the entire stock in trade of its owner, a water vender. Yet one need not necessarily go far to find a treasure. We one day secured a most shapely jar, eighteen inches high and of early Pennsylvania make, through a glimpse of it turned upside down on the picket of a fence, just a couple of miles from our home. And the owner did not care for it in the least.

We find ourselves writing almost as much of what was put into the rooms as of the rooms themselves; and, indeed, furnishing and decorating are a vital part of home-making. Quite as important as to have proper rooms, is to have proper things for the rooms—and it adds a keen zest when the things have not only fitness of shape and color, but the charm of personal experiences and old-time association besides.

On the side wall of the chimney-breast was one of the old-fashioned fireplace cupboards, with a solid wooden door. It opened from the side, just where the two steps mount through the thick stone wall of the original house to the library, and was merely a hiding place. But the idea came that this was the proper abiding place for some old china; proper, after a simple alteration should be made. For one

wants a shelved place for old china, but at the
same time a place where the treasures may be
seen; it ought not to be cluttered on tables or
mantels, but it ought not to be hidden away;
and here was a chance:—for it was no trouble
at all to put some panes of glass in place of the
solid panels of the door, and thus give opportunity to see, on the three shelves within, some
little cream jugs, some old luster, some Sunder-
land, some Lowestoft, some Sèvres.

On the mahogany door opening into the
hall, put in to replace a door of pine with badly
"alligatored" graining and white crockery door-
knobs, we put a pair of old brass door-knobs, of
the rare rayed and oval shape, that had been
offered to us for twenty-five cents at a house
in the heart of New York City. Whenever the
home-maker sees brass door-knobs, whether on
the stand of a junkman, the bench of a village
carpenter, or in a building being destroyed, they
should be secured and put away for use, for
they add value and distinction, and are becoming more expensive and hard to find.

These rayed and oval knobs are really things
of special beauty. And, after all, why shouldn't
a host of little things be fine, that modern laxity

and haste and the convenience of crude castings have permitted to drift into cheapness and insignificance! The hand of Michael Angelo, "the hand that rounded Peter's dome," also traced designs of beautiful doorknobs.

When we took this house we possessed more than a dozen brass door-knobs which had been obtained at various times and places. Chancing to stop at a stock farm, one day, there seemed to be something unusual about the handle of an awl that the farmer was holding in his hand.

"Isn't that handle a brass door-knob?"

"Yep; made it to punch holes in bulls' noses." The man's manner was dour and reckless. "Care for it? Take it! You can have it"— recklessness tempered by thrift—"for ten cents."

As he pocketed the ten cents he went on moodily: "You can buy anything on the place. I'm getting rid of every dinged thing. You see"— growing morosely confidential—"my wife, she's run away. But she'll come back, and when she comes I want her not to find a dodgasted thing!"

A successful finishing touch not only adds character to this particular room, but also seems to help the entire house. And yet it was a thing most simply and briefly done, after the room was finished, and was put on as an after-thought. It was merely the placing of a "broken pediment" over the door; a pediment being the classical triangular decoration over porticos or doorways, which, since the time of Queen Anne, has even more commonly been used with a "broken" or open space taking the place of the upper point, and there being there a rounded-out opening, usually with a vertical ornament in its center.

The molding across the upper part of the door was taken off and cut in half. A plain, flat, gable-shaped board was fitted on the wall, flush with the flat part of the casing, above the door. The two halves, mitered properly where they left the casing, and with their upper ends cut with the curve of the rounded-out opening, were then set up to make a raking cornice. They did not meet, in the center, by several inches, and in the center of the rounded-out opening, and rising slightly above the open "break," was set a small formal torch, carved in wood.

When painted, all this looked as if it had always been there; as, indeed, it might well have

AN EXPERIMENT WITH A PEDIMENT

been, as it goes naturally with houses of this type.

And, best of all, the work took but the labor of two hours to complete!—making, thus, still another result given by slight effort. Not to "despise the day of small things" was the sage admonition of the ancient prophet.

CHAPTER VI

A WHITE-PANELED DINING-ROOM

MEANWHILE, the days and the weeks were passing; for such work must needs be slow, done as we were doing it. And, too, there were the demands of one's regular occupation; it was far from being a case of having nothing to do but to plan and supervise and change. And there were the general demands upon time that come from daily care of a home and grounds; there were the daily matters of the household; there was the garden; and always, besides the particular room definitely in hand, there was more or less of matters regarding other parts of the house, and at all times a considerable amount of work with lawn and shrubs and general out-of-doors. And there were the usual amenities of life: for we saw that we were to be quite a while in completing the house and there seemed to be no good reason why we should meanwhile consider ourselves shut out of the zone of friend-liness.

A WHITE-PANELED DINING-ROOM

It was neither deterrent, restraining, nor cause for regret, that it was really hard work for us and that there was considerable inconvenience involved, for the gradual attaining of results and the glowing promise of still further results were fully compensatory.

Although many changes were made, and, in some of the rooms, extensive changes, it was never for the mere sake of changing, never from a belief that a change is good from the mere fact of being a change. If a room or a house is just right it ought to remain as it is; and in the case of such a room or such a house there would be ample scope for the expression of the home-maker's individuality in decoration and furniture. But as a matter of fact it is incredible that any house should in every respect conform to the ideas, desires, standards, of any one who is accustomed to think and plan and judge for himself. And although it is true that changes ought not to be made for the mere sake of changing, it is also true that changes, planned and carried out by yourself, make your home peculiarly your own home, in a close and intimate way. Hawthorne somewhere writes of the joy that comes from watching the growth of the vegetables you have planted; a joy that arises from your sense of having taken part in the process of creation: and, this being true in regard to a single adjunct of home-making, and a creation in which, after all, the human part is necessarily minor, how much keener is the joy of watching the growth of the home itself, when you have so taken part in its creation as actually to plan and control its growth in every detail!

Concerning the dining-room, our hopes were high, although, to begin with, the room as we found it had scarcely a single one of the points which a good dining-room ought to have. It was, indeed, well lighted; but even this virtue was not a virtue, for the altering of the windows was one of the imperative necessities.

A dining-room deserves special consideration; for, although only a small part of each day is spent there, it is a very important part. Good digestion is far more likely to wait on appetite if the appetite is satisfied in a room where mind and eye and body are alike rested and pleased. A dining-room ought to be not only comfortable, but attractive; not only attractive, but comfortable.

To begin with, we visualized what we wished

the dining-room to be, and made a mental picture of what we hoped for as the general result:— a square room with a round table in the center; a square room paneled, with a bank of windows and a fireplace. That the room was far from square, and had neither panels nor a fireplace nor bank of windows, were not permitted to be prohibitive considerations. Over and over again it should be urged that your rooms can be made and should be made to develop up to their possibilities. The important thing is to make the mental picture and then go ahead and make the picture real. In home-making one must get his facts from his imagination.

A dining-room ought to be practically square because it is a room in which everything happens in the middle. There ought to be a fireplace, not as sole reliance for heating, but to give an air of comfort, of cheer, of homelikeness. And nothing is so effective as paneling, for even the best of wall-paper is far from equaling it in appearance and dignity.

As we found it, the dining-room was seventeen feet six by fourteen feet six, and the length was increased by a bay-window of peculiar unsightliness. The room was separated from the kitchen by a serving pantry which was far from necessary, and which was seventeen feet six by four and a half feet. The natural and obvious thing to do was to take down the partition between pantry and dining-room and take off the bay window, and thus have a dining-room seventeen feet six by nineteen feet. This possibility again showed that advantages accrue from having a house a little larger than one's absolute needs; that advantages come from having somewhat of leeway in alterations.

The taking down of the partition and the merging of the two spaces was an easy task. Fortunately, the partition rested on the floor, so there was no floor patching necessary; but even if it had gone right through the floor the subsequent repairing would not have been at all serious. It can not too often be insisted upon that partitions should seldom be allowed to stand in the way of improvements.

There was an outfit of pipes and faucets and sink for the washing of dishes in that pantry, and, with the partition down, these were now in the dining-room and in full view. They must, therefore, be taken out. At the same time it would be foolish to do away with expensive plumbing

THE WHITE-PANELED DINING-ROOM

and piping if it could readily be used in some other way. The pipes came up on one side of a partition wall running down into the cellar. A plumber turned them up on the other side of the wall, so as to emerge in the kitchen. There a carpenter rearranged the dripboards, and thus this plumbing was made a matter of use and convenience, supplementary to the other faucets and sink already in the kitchen, and at a total cost of only five dollars and a half.

And to this there was an odd and unexpected sequel. Some time afterward, when a gas cooking-range was to be set in the kitchen, there was no good place for it except where the original kitchen sink stood, and it was clearly evident that the sink could be taken out and the gas stove given its place, through the presence of the better sink and faucets so opportunely put in from the vanished serving-pantry. The hero of one of Anthony Hope's novels, when told that a certain result had come from luck, calmly replied that he considered luck one of his resources; and luck may certainly be counted upon as one of the resources of the home-maker who goes at his work with confidence.

The serving pantry had a window which now

came in a corner of the dining-room—not where it ought to be; therefore, it was taken out and the wall closed with lath and plaster, a matter of but a few hours' work. Such changes are easily made, especially when other rough structural work is in progress.

The big bay window, ugly, awkward, ungraceful, square-angled, was on the same side of the room and ran up to the second story. Externally, it was even worse than on the inside, and so it had to be taken out and the space closed up. To give the best effect to that side of the room, a bank of three windows, flush with the wall instead of projecting like the bay, was to be put in, and as they did not precisely measure the same width as the demolished bay, and as, besides this, the bay window space was not in the middle of the wall of the new-made room, this required further manipulation of the wall.

The bank of three windows was ordered of heavy and solid construction and of a size to reach from the cornice-line to just seventeen inches above the floor, at which height a window-seat was to be built. It is astonishing what character and effectiveness are gained by having windows come so low. It is one of the greatest mistakes to have the base of a window high above the floor unless there is some special local or structural reason for it. And it was particularly desirable here to have the windows low, as on this side of the house the ground drops away in a long slope, making an attractive little view down through trees and greenery to the spring-house and where there was to be a pool.

The panes in the three big banked windows are small; eight by eleven; and there are twenty-four in the center one and eighteen in each of the sides. Small panes are usually so effective in themselves, and they harmonize with Colonial effects so much better than do larger ones, that there was no hesitation about having them. A bank of sixty window-panes, heavy sashed, and eight by eleven, could scarcely fail to look well.

No window-sill was made at the base of these windows, the place of sills being taken by the long, flat board of the window-seat. It would be a mistake to have both window-seat and sills. A long window-seat is always admirable in a dining-room, as it gives extra seating capacity when needed for some gathering of one's friends, as for a tea or supper. The window-seat was made of the proper-looking and at the same time sufficiently comfortable width of fourteen inches—sufficiently comfortable, for one does not wish to see, in a dining-room, any seat particularly easy or reposeful. A chair or a seat ought always to be comfortable; but different rooms have different standards of comfort; and that of a dining-room ought to tend toward the perpendicular. Even the arm-chair in a dining-room is not, properly, quite so comfortable as the fireside chair of a library. And this window-seat has always been kept as a long plain seat, without cushions or pillows. In winter-time it is an admirable place for the setting of two small formal box bushes.

In the corner of the dining-room, where it opened into the kitchen, there was a very bad break in the line of the room; a clumsy awk-ward-looking recess from which opened not only the door into the kitchen but also one upon the rear stairway; this latter door having the additional disadvantage, from the point of looks, of swinging into the room at the step level of seven inches above the floor. It was an ill-favored combination and there was much cogitation as to the best means of correcting it. A grille and a pair of curtains suggested themselves, but such a remedy would have been worse than the disease. For a time, there seemed nothing more feasible than a partition and a door, although that would have made a dark and tiny hallway.

It was while one plan after another for remedying this really important defect was being mulled over, and while the wall for the bank of windows was being carpentered into shape, that a pair of glass doors dropped in with entire unexpectedness and were joyfully seized upon as offering and being the desired solution.

To be sure, they did not look like glass doors when we first saw them. It might easily have been a case of entertaining glass doors unawares.

It came about in this way. The mill, in getting out the windows—the set of three for this room and a set of three for the room above, where the bay window was also removed—made the mistake of making the two side ones shorter than the one in the middle. Because the measurements were given in that way for the up-stairs three they made the dining-room three on a similar plan. When told of it they at once acknowledged their error. "We'll send the right size," they wrote. "And don't bother about sending back the wrong ones.   Just throw them away."

Then it was that the inspiration came. These two windows, placed side by side, just filled the width of the broken corner and were ideal for a pair of glass doors! Their panes, they having been made for this room, were of the same size as those in the big new windows—another fortunate point.   They were not, however, tall enough—only four feet; and so, to put two feet of length on the bottom, a door with three sets of panels was sawed in part, and the upper two and lower two panels used, two under each side, and made structurally complete by means of strips of wood.   It was another of the numberless fortuitous chances that come to hopeful homemakers that the four narrow panels were easily fitted to the width of the two frames of glass, and that thus there came glass doors whose lower part was wood.   Said the carpenter wonderingly: "That is the only door I ever saw that had top panels and bottom panels just alike in size!"   And it is really quite uncommon, although not quite so uncommon as he thought.

Above the evolved glass doors was placed an ancient "halfmoon" window which we had acquired a year or two before and had been holding for some good use to arise. The corner was now entirely satisfactory, with a fine Georgian effect, and looked as if it had been originally built and planned in just that way. It left, between dining-room and kitchen, a little glassed-in space large enough to comply with Viollet-le-Duc's dictum that there should never be direct communication between these two rooms, but always some kind of intermediate space to minimize kitchen smells and sounds.

The irregular step at the foot of the rear stairs was now completely out of sight and the glass doors left precisely to an inch the right space for the door at the foot of the stairs to swing open—another of the numberless fortunate chances.

And against the wall, within that narrow space at the foot of stairs, were set, on edge, on narrow strips, five rows of old-time blue plates, which show through to the dining-room in a softly genial glow. The narrow strips on which the plates sit were pieces of the discarded electric-wire channels from the ceilings, and for their new purpose nothing could be better.

Between dining-room and hall were two doors, which, happening to be of pine, were taken off and replaced with doors of old mahogany, refinished and polished and fitted with handles of brass.

A cornice was one of the necessities, and so one was put in. Almost any good room is better for a cornice. It used to be that almost all well-made houses were thus built, but cornices gradually fell into disuse through the overornateness and lowering of taste of half a century ago, and also through the coming into general use of wall-paper borders. When borders were put under cornices people began to see that they didn't go well together—and so, discarding the right and holding to the wrong, they did without cornices! Now, the taste is gradually swinging back to cornices again and to questioning the desirability of borders.

For this room we wanted a plain, good-looking cornice with very simple curves; and we saw the plainness, the good looks, and the simplicity of curve in some ready-made cornice made to go under the eaves of a common porch. It cost three cents a foot, was four and a half inches in depth, and was precisely the thing, except that the depth was not quite sufficient in proportion to the height of the room. But deepened by a strip of plain wood fastened against the wall for a depth of two and a half inches—making thus a total cornice depth of seven inches —it was precisely what the room needed. It was a cornice of attractive lines with the desired charm and simplicity of Georgian effect.

As to the fireplace, that we looked upon as a needful concomitant of a dining-room—well, there was no fireplace in the room. It needed to be in the center of the wall, directly facing the three windows; the wall being an extremely thick one, of stone. Fortunately there was a chimney in the wall, although it had never been opened into the dining-room; it opened instead, into the hall, by means of a fireplace. Well, there was no real reason why the same chimney should not be made to do for two fireplaces— it would only mean that both could not have a fire at the same time, and this would be no hardship in a house relying upon furnace heat; and so, the wall was opened and an old-fashioned mantel of cream-white marble set in place with a hearth of plain bricks, set on edge in herring-bone design. And for the very trifling sum of seven cents a letter, twenty-eight cents in all—and the cost is mentioned to show, as many things show, that to realize a pleasant thought need not necessarily demand much money—our initials, in tile letters, of the same color as the brick, and four inches long, were bought, and laid in as part of the hearth, on either side of the fireplace.

That this mantel came six hundred miles to us and had been, on account of personal associations, saved for us for some years after the tearing down of the house in which it had originally stood, only shows what pleasant things can be done with a house.

From the first, it had been decided that this room was to be white; and from the first it was to be paneled. A white-paneled dining-room!—the idea had always been fascinating, and so why should it not be carried out?

But paneling costs much money. And the key-note of our work was, from the first, comparative inexpensiveness, for, as with the majority of Americans, questions of cost had constantly to be considered. Well, then, it followed that the paneling must be done inexpensively.

It is really very curious that paneling fell so

much into disuse in this country. Many of the old-time ordinary town or country houses were charmingly paneled without any idea of pretentiousness or of anything unusual. It was the exigencies and limitations of our early and hurried national life that took Americans from the best standards, but in many respects, including this of paneling, there is a growing tendency to return to the best things.

Material for the lower part of the room had opportunely offered itself after the house alterations were well under way; this material being quite a number of ancient, narrow cupboard doors from the sides of the fireplace of an old house that was being torn down. These old panels, some white, some grained, some red, had been piled up on our back porch in shabby retirement, and with little of promise about them to eyes not ours.

In England old paneling material is eagerly watched for when old structures are being destroyed. Church pews, ship cabins, and the like furnish forth many a modern mansion with wainscot paneling; but in our own country all such material is usually wasted, though inside shutters when solid, not slatted, and even the fronts of

9 [129]

some shop counters, and frequently finely paneled doors, may be acquired by him who has use for them.

The cupboard doors were not to panel the entire room; they were to make a paneled wainscot two and a half feet high, and above that there was to be paneling of a totally different kind.

The raised rectangles of the doors—the parts that were to be used in paneling—were of extremely variant sizes. Almost every one of the doors had three rectangles of graduated lengths: a square at the top, a larger panel in the middle, and a still longer one at the bottom. Nor was this all; for the doors themselves, being from different rooms and different fireplaces, were of different sizes.

Looking back, in retrospect, at the pile of paint-marred, odd-sized, uneven cupboard doors, we can not feel surprised that the carpenter gazed at it in hopeless incomprehension when told that it was to be white paneling; and so it was necessary, over night, to study and measure and shift and balance and arrange and have it all ready in numbered order for him to begin work with in the morning.

LOWER PANELING, MADE FROM OLD CUPBOARD DOORS; UPPER PANELING, MADE FROM NARROW MOLDING, ON DECORATOR'S CANVAS

A WHITE-PANELED DINING-ROOM

When it was finished, the effect was very much better than as if the rectangles for paneling had been all of a size. By using the narrow ones under each window, by balancing pairs in corners, by mating them between windows and in the other wall spaces, there was none of that general effect as if it were ready-made and cut by the running yard. As it is, it seems made for this particular room—as if each piece had been made for its particular spot—and in this air of having been built specially for its location lies a great part of the charm of all properly-made paneling.

Had our paneling material been wider it could have reached its height of two and a half feet and, at the same time, have gone clear to the floor without a baseboard. If one were to use new material the baseboard should be eliminated. But as it was, the first operation in the panel-work was to block out the baseboard just so far as to make it rest against the paneling as it formerly rested against the plaster of the wall.

Between the wainscot paneling and the cornice was now five feet of space; and this broad space was to be covered with the other paneling planned for.

First, the entire bare space was spread with what is known as decorator's canvas; a strong, stiff, prepared, white fabric, which can be pasted right on the wall, and which need never show seams where its widths come together, because, when the edges are cut and butted, putty may be so used as to obliterate every sign of a joint. At the top the canvas was pushed under the cornice, that having been left loose until this was done, and at the bottom it was pushed under the finish of the wainscot paneling above described, which was already in place.

Decorator's canvas costs twenty-five cents a square yard and, when properly painted, gives a surface precisely like wood in appearance.

This was now all spaced off, in panel-shaped rectangles (each with its corners squarely mitered and returned), by means of three-quarter-inch angle molding, of pine, nailed lightly on. This molding cost but a cent a foot: certainly cheap enough, though it was amusing to notice that it took as many feet as a pair of centipedes.

In the spacing, the determining of the sizes of the panels, lies the important secret of good paneling: what might, indeed, be called its vital principle. For the sizes and spacing depend

upon what is technically known as the "stile";
that is, the open space around each panel.

From the top of the wainscot paneling to
the bottom of the cornice was five feet. To
make each panel four feet in height would
leave six inches for the "stile" at the top and
at the bottom. In the arranging of the panels
there were widely-different spaces to put them
in; between door and window, between fireplace and door, on the long wall where the sideboard was to stand, in the narrow space between
door and corner, and so on. But, however the
width of panel should vary to fit the space, the
height was fixed, always the same. Nor was
this all. The six-inch "stile" must be preserved
at each side as well as at top and bottom. Each
panel must be surrounded by its "stile" space.
Between the side of a panel and a door or fireplace must be six inches, but between the side
of one panel and the side of another panel
the apparent anomaly of twelve inches; and
this because the eye demands that each panel
have its individual space.

When all was done the wall was painted
white. Ordinary paint would not give the
desired soft, unvarnished effect, especially on

decorator's canvas, and therefore a special, but not expensive, flat-finish paint was used; a paint which gives admirable finish with only two coats and which is guaranteed to retain its fine white color for years.

And so it was all done; done so simply, so easily, so inexpensively; and the entire room has all the desired appearance of being paneled in wood.

Nor need even the most rigid-minded deem such things to have in them anything of deceit, for it is neither deceit nor pretense when one endeavors to follow a beautiful ideal and, not being able to follow it along the usual moneyed road, goes economically along the path he can afford to travel. The test is altogether in one's own mind.

Paneling is arbitrary in its control of pictures. There can not be indiscriminate hanging of them in a paneled room, for the lines and spaces control their location. Yet this is not a defect. Restraint adds to effectiveness.

In this dining-room there are only two places to hang pictures; and there are only two pictures hung. One is a portrait in which the predominant color is a soft red, which harmonizes excellently with the white of the room—perhaps because it is of that supposedly impossible "cool" red; and this is remindful of a decorator who, challenged in his statement that red could be cool, replied triumphantly with the suggestion of crushed strawberries in ice. The other picture is also a painting, a portrait, and is still in its old-time frame of dull gold. One has the vantage point over the fireplace and the other looks out, into the room, across the sideboard.

In the center of each of the other panels is placed an ancient candle-bracket of plain and attractive design, as we were once so fortunate as to obtain quite a number from two little pre-Revolutionary churches which had long since discarded them to the cellar. Candle light is the most soft and charming of lights for dining; yet candle-brackets can readily be used with electricity should one prefer. And for those who do not happen to hit upon once becandled churches with bracket treasure still recoverable, it may be mentioned that excellent candle-brackets are on the market at reasonable prices, perhaps the best being made in the little brass-workers' shops of the Russians, in New York.

The sideboard is of mahogany, a great long treasure of a Heppelwhite that we had found at an old house in New Jersey; in the corner is an old corner cupboard, and the dining-table is a Sheraton whose reeded legs are a spur to decorative ambition: "You will certainly have to live up to those table-legs!" as a friend expressed it. On the mantel were placed only a pair of tall brass candlesticks whose candles burn on a line with those in the brackets, and a jug of old and curious ware, of rich and subdued colors. And the furnishings are mentioned because the character and looks of what is put into a room are quite as important as the looks and character of the room itself. "You catch sight of something on the mantel that gives the whole thing away!" as Whistler once expressed it.

Not till the very last, after we thought the room complete, did a certain solitary table-leg do its part.

That table-leg had given our friends cause for joyful gibing. It had been picked up for a few cents because it was such a good-looking table-leg! But what, we were asked, could **we** do with one solitary, lone, single table-leg?

A WHITE-PANELED DINING-ROOM

What, indeed! Really, there wasn't any very tangible excuse for having it. But one day there came the idea of where to build a much-needed china cupboard, and with it the picture of its being a mahogany-pilastered cupboard; and what could be better for two mahogany pilasters than a mahogany table-leg sawed through its length?

Well, perhaps, something better than one table-leg would be two table-legs. And while planning the scheme, there arrived a second table-leg, this one from a friend who thought our pride in the possession of one was so diverting that he had cut off a leg from an ancient five-legged table that he owned—thinking four legs enough for any table!—and sent it along. The two legs were not a match in girth; one was fat and one was lean; but they were alike in being of Empire design, with twisted rope and acanthus, and so they would go perfectly together as pilasters, though not as legs.

Between dining-room and hall were two doorways. One was necessity, the other was surplusage. The partition wall was eighteen inches deep, it having been the outside wall of the original house, the dining-room having been built on later. And the idea was to put an Empire pilastered china closet in that door space, leaving the old mahogany door to close it in.

Sides and top were fronted with an arching piece of mahogany cut from a mahogany board, and a keystone of mahogany was set at the top in the center. Scallop-fronted pine shelves were put in. All the shelving and the back and sides were painted white. Then down the front were set the long pilasters, each side made of half a leg of the fat one at the bottom and half a leg of the lean one at the top. It was really quite Tennysonian: Half a leg, half a leg, half a leg onward!

THE CUPBOARD OF THE TABLE LEGS

CHAPTER VII

THE HALLS OF THE HOUSE

THE hall is a difficult part of the house to plan properly, arrange properly, alter properly. And yet, the matter is greatly simplified if, from the first, it is kept in mind that a hall must be hospitable and that it is essentially a passageway; that it is a place in which people are to be met; not primarily a place for converse and sociability. Although right here an important difference between the lower and the upper halls may be suggested. The two, in arrangement, must needs be part of one connected scheme, and both are essentially passageways, but although the lower hall should not be made a sitting-room, the upper hall may easily be a most admirable one.

Important though the entrance hall is, in its effect on the visitor and the impression, good or bad, that it gives of the entire house, whether of good taste or bad, whether of hospitality or the reverse, whether individual or commonplace, it is curious that, in the description of houses even by men of infinite detail, it is so often overlooked, ignored, made little or nothing of. A host of examples might be adduced. Take the house of Mr. Wickfield in Canterbury: Dickens lingers lovingly over its exterior, with multitudinous particularity, and then suddenly sets the reader within the long, low parlor. And when the House of the Seven Gables is pictured as proudly thrown open to the first guests, the reader is given a long and fascinating description of exterior details and then, with a word, is shown through the hall into one or another of the rooms. The outside appearance of the Wayside Inn is given ample description, and then you find yourself within the wainscoted parlor, without any notice taken of the spacious hall, full of beauty and dignity as it is.

It is fortunate if the home-maker finds the hall precisely to his mind, for it is likely to be the most difficult part of the house to alter; so difficult, in fact, that even the most sanguine may be given pause.

It is ordinarily a simple matter to alter a room, even though it involves the changing of partitions and windows and doors. But to alter a hall usually means, in the first place, an expensive altering of the stair—for, although it is easy to take out a stair entirely and close the gap, it is costly to alter the shape of a stair, or its position, or the rise and tread of the steps, or the headroom. . But much more important is the fact that changes in a hall involve changes and new conditions on two floors instead of merely on one. Plan a change which will work out admirably for the first floor and you will be confronted with unexpected problems for the second. Plan changes which will make a marked improvement in the second floor and you will be faced with unexpected questions of interdependence in regard to lower hall and dining-room or parlor. As a matter of fact, our own hall stands in some respects as an example of how not to have it, and this in spite of the fact that we are enthusiasts for changing whatever ought to be changed and, from experience, optimistic as to the ease with which changes can be made. The point of importance with one's hall is, if it is necessary to leave some things in not the ideally best form, to have it at least representative and of proper effect—

in other words, to rise superior to unavoidable defects.

In the first place, the ideal front door is heavy and broad and solid and thick. Its use is not solely to let people in, but also to keep people out. It is a bulwark as well as an entrance; it should be heavy but not inhospitable. Just such a door we found in place, as old as the central portion of the house—older, that is, than the Revolution—and it is recessed within the thick stone wall, and paneled in the recess, and has a row of little panes overhead. Nowadays doors are tall and narrow—most are mill-made, and the mills set this tall and narrow fashion—but in the older days it was held as a canon of the best building that the width of a door should be half its height. This door almost follows that good, old-fashioned rule, for it is three feet five by six feet five, and it would have been the necessary trifle higher had not the old-time builder taken into consideration the effect of the little row of overhead glass panes.

But, fitting and delightful though the door was, it was not quite at its best. It had had, in the old days, a great door-latch—the marks were still there—but some would-be improver without fear of the god of good taste before his eyes, had taken it off and put in its place a crockery knob. Fortunately, we had a fine brass latch from an old house in that town of beautiful old houses, Portsmouth, and put it on. The door, unlike most old doors of its period, had never had a knocker, but we happened to have an old one of brass which gave precisely the needful touch of finish.

Ordinarily, the hallway is the room from which the main stairway goes up-stairs. For ourselves, we believe that happy is the hall in which the stair does not instantly confront the person entering, as if it had been lying in wait for him. When the stair is set back from the door, neither messengers nor casual callers are faced with what seems an invitation to ascend; and there is ample room for the formal and cordial welcome of guests. There is no better example of what a stair in a hall ought to be than that at Mt. Vernon; it is charming and dignified in every detail, and is set back well away from the front door, where it adds beauty and dignity of its own to the general effect.

In our house we found the foot of the stair

close to the front door, and there was a general effect of narrowness on account of the size and clumsiness of newel post and balusters, ugly interlopers of the seventies. For quite a while we earnestly hoped to be able to set the stair farther back, for the squarish shape of the hall— seventeen feet by fourteen—made it seem feasible. However, it was not quite feasible, without altogether too much of expense, but still there was much that could be done.

First of all, the stair was widened in reality, and still more widened in general effect, by taking out the big balusters and replacing them with the slender, graceful Colonial balusters and newels and rail that we had secured from an ancient, demolished house, as already told; and it was astonishing what grace and general effectiveness were gained.

But it came to us, some time after this stair alteration was finished, that we had failed to please everybody; that, in fact, we had failed to please the carpenter who had done the work of alteration!—for he said to some one, and in due time it filtered its way along: "You remember that house? Well, there's some people there just spoiling it. They've torn the house to bits! They've taken out—yes, sir!—the best sort of a modern oak baluster and some fine oak mantels and hunted up some old things to put in place instead. Why, sir, they've set back that house a hundred years!"

The stair turned at a landing beneath a deep-silled window, and at the right were a step and a door leading to a garret stair. Nothing was more superfluous than that stair, for in the back hall was another garret stair, and nothing could be more awkward than the superfluous stair and the entire arrangement, and so the step and door and stair were removed, and the wall lathed and plastered. In all, there was a great gain in both dignity and simplicity —two qualities closely related in architecture and decoration—and when the stairs, left bare as hall stairs ought to be, were scraped and waxed, they did not seem to have the faults that had originally confronted us.

The floor of the hall was of hardwood; and a hardwood floor with a rug is about as good a combination as can be had. At the same time, if one is building a new house it would be well to consider a hall floor of brick or tile, such as is often used in Germany and France, and as was not infrequently used in American houses previous to 1750; as witness the hospitable, white wainscoted hall of Stenton, warmed by the homely glow of the dull red bricks of its floor. However, American builders of to-day do not favor brick or tile, and in our own case, even had there not been a good floor of hardwood, needful support for brick or tile would have required special construction.

There was a fireplace at one side of the hall. Now, ordinarily, it seems unfitting to have a fireplace in the lower hall, it not being a sitting-room. But there the fireplace was, and, on the whole, it seemed better to leave it there. Should we ever think differently, it could readily be taken out. But we set no chair, no bench beside it—we aimed at no inglenook effect. A square hall does not offer the objections to a fireplace that a narrow hall does, if all appearance of making it a gathering-spot is avoided.

However, the fireplace is not precisely as we found it. It was framed in a mantel-piece of those unfortunate seventies, the original mantel having been taken out and thrown away, and there was nothing for it but for us to take out this in turn. And a fitting one to take its place—for in house alterations everything comes to him who looks for it—came with pleasant promptitude. We were walking together past a large auction shop in the large city at whose edge we had found our home, and in its outer cellar stair lay just the ancient mantel we needed. It was to be sold the next day at auction, but two dollars at once secured it, delivered at the railway station—a thing of fine lines and shapeliness, of just the proper size and of the proper period.

The building into one house of fine material from some other house, is not done, in America, to nearly the extent that it ought to be, although more and more are awakening to the possibilities. Art lovers among the wealthy have had entire ceilings taken out of palaces in Italy and built into palaces in America; the late Stanford White, with his splendid taste and the wealth at his command, transferred many a beautiful mantel, many a pillar and balcony, many a bit of cornice; others, without wealth, have secured and used fine details; the finest doorway in ancient Deerfield was taken there from an old house that was being demolished in old Greenwich Village, in New York City; and two new New York hotels secured cheaply, for their reception rooms, superb mantels from the Stewart mansion in what was long ago known as De Pauw Row. Old and fine mantels, in fact, can still be readily found. Many an old house is torn down and its mantels and moldings thrown away as rubbish to be picked up if anybody cares for them. A friend, an architect, looking from his office window the other day, saw an old colored man staggering down the street under the weight of a mantel. The architect knew a good thing when he saw it. "I'll give you ten dollars for that," he shouted down, only to receive the discouraging response: "Already sold, suh; sorry, suh; got fifteen, suh"; which makes us still more pleased with our own purchase.

A clock seems necessary in an entrance hall; and although one may ordinarily want but little here below, he wants that clock long. Really, the tall clock, of "grandfather's" shape, is peculiarly adapted to almost any hall. When the hall stairway turns at a landing which is not more than half the height of the stair that is a good place to set the clock. In this hall the stair turn is near the top, and so the clock,

THE LOWER HALL, WITH TRANSPLANTED BALUSTERS AND RAIL

which happens to be an ancient one, with wooden works, was not set there, but beside the fireplace.

Above the mantel-piece is a long mirror, Empire in design, paneled in three parts. Now, we had never intended to have a long mirror over a hall mantel-piece, but this old mirror so precisely fitted the old mantel that it was set up experimentally, and soon came to be appreciated for its obvious utility, for it permits several at a time to settle the eternal question of whether or not their hats are on straight.

A solid table, rather long and rather narrow, standing against the wall, holds the transient hat and coat and takes the place of the tentacled terror of the hatrack.

A hall should never be treated as a storeroom. It is not the place to set out an assortment of laprobes, hammocks, raincoats, rubber overshoes, dropped in corners, draped on chairs, hung on hooks. Convenience is one of the false gods. Doctor Bovary had a bridle behind the hall door and a pair of muddy leggings in a corner, but Madame Bovary would have thought more of him if he hadn't been that kind of man.

Do you remember the delightful old "powdering-rooms," spoken of familiarly in many a novel of old-time life? Well, the "powdering-room" was a little room just off the lower hall, into which a guest could slip for a final look at a mirror and a final touch of powder—for the hair, in those days, rather than the face—before entering the general gathering-rooms. Such a little room, retaining or not its old-time designation, is extremely convenient at the side of any hall; so convenient, in fact, that it is well worth some trouble to arrange, for it is so pleasant to have a room for the final touch to the toilet, the final primping, where one can be away from the full publicity of the hall. And here is how such a room was made.

Under the stairway was a space devoted to a stair which led down into the cellar. It was a bad place for a cellar stair—ingenuity could hardly contrive a worse; and, more than that, it was certainly surplusage, for there was another stair leading down from the kitchen. So the stair from the hall was boarded over; and then it came to us that here was the "powdering-room."

Indeed, nothing could be more ideal, for a

large window opens into it from the rear porch, giving plentiful light.

The closet is not cramped in height, for although it decreases with the descending hall stair above it, it is quite high enough for anybody under the upper steps, and has also the high and level space under the high landing. Set in this adaptation of a "powdering-room" are a chair, a little table, and a mirror; and, in all, it could not be more satisfactory if it had been especially planned for its present primping purpose at the time of the building of the house. And this is described—the purpose can not be too often repeated—to show not merely the advantages of a little, lighted, mirrored room in down-stairs accessibility, just off the hall, but to show that one should always be on the lookout to find some better use for a space than that space has been heretofore devoted to. That a space given up to the sole purpose of a useless cellarway could, with scarcely any trouble, be made into really delightful usefulness, is typical and illustrative of the possibilities that lie before any householder.

Such a room is a most advantageous place

to have running water, and many a house is nowadays built with it there.

Opening from the hall upon a retired nook of a back porch—a porch which we were to pave with brick and beyond which we were to lay out a flowered and low-walled garden—was a doorway, in which were two sets of narrow, middle-opening doors, one set outside of the other. The outer two were of solid wood —useful for protection, but not ornamental— and the inner two were fly-screen doors. But we were not quite satisfied. And when, in a dusty corner of the roomy garret, there was found a pair of glass doors, we were impatient till they could be tested in this place. And they belonged to it! And while wondering that these doors should ever have been put away out of sight in the garret, we felt under obligation to the owner of some past year for not having thrown them away; for now from within the hall one looks right out upon the garden through this French-windowed door space.

But there need be no idea that French doors, or French windows as they are often called, are deemed admirable because they are French; it is only because they are admirable. If they were American or Italian or any other kind they would be just the same; for French doors by any other name would look as sweet.

Above these French doors a little transomed nook formed itself which was just the place for a few pieces of Flemish pottery; for it is a theory of furnishing that gives good results, that decorative articles such as these should not be scattered throughout a house, but segregated in groups wherever possible.

In color the hall was left very light, with mantel-piece, window frames, and balusters painted white, and a wall-paper of soft buff with narrow and almost indistinguishable stripe. The stair rail itself and the doors retained their natural color of mahogany; and this, not only because of the attractiveness of the combination of mahogany and white, but also from the practical utility of not having those things white which are frequently to be touched with the hands.

The white window-frames and the light buff wall-paper and the mahogany doors are for the upper hall as well as the lower, the two halls being as much a part of the same scheme of decoration as if they were parts of the same room on the same floor. The light buff paper was chosen as a good background for some old prints, Napoleonic and English, set within cream-colored mats and the narrowest of black frames. Similar old prints ascend with the stairs and encompass the upper hall.

The charming ramp of the staircase should always be preserved if, like ourselves, you are adjusting ancient balusters and rail—the ramp being that fetching shape, bend, curve, where the rail moves upward to the top to enter the post at right angles. It seems incredible that so positively beautiful a thing as a ramp should have come to be disused in the building of most modern homes.

Although it should never be forgotten that the upper hall, like the lower, is essentially a passageway, a place from which other rooms may be reached, it ought, if possible, to be much more. It ought to be a place for informal meetings, a tête-à-tête room, a room for brief and pleasant talks, a place where, without any appearance of design, two or three may gather together for that pleasant kind of chat that comes from the informal meeting of friends or members of the family. It should be a place to sit down in with a book; a place to sew in; a place to rest in. In short, it may be made into a room almost indispensable, but its character and its interest and its effectiveness would be materially lessened if it were formally considered as a sitting-room and treated as such.

To get the best use from an up-stairs hall it ought, therefore, to be of fair size; something more than the narrow passage that it is in so many houses. In this house, we found it already built as practically a room, of precisely the size of the hall below, opening conveniently to the bedrooms and with the extremely useful concomitant of a passage leading from it to storeroom and bathroom.

An old long sofa at one side seemed both inevitable and ideal; a chair or so, a full-length mirror between the windows close to the head of the stairs—an unselfish sort of a place for a long mirror for all to use, for the final reviewing glance of those going down—and an old-time desk, with ink and pens and paper always ready to the hand. This last is really a great convenience, obviating the necessity of having a desk in any of the bedrooms, and at the same time making it unnecessary for a

guest or one of the family to go to the library
to write a letter or make memoranda. Until
a desk in such a place is actually tried it is
impossible to realize its great usefulness and
varied convenience. Here also stands the telephone.

And that this hall is in the pre-Revolutionary
part of the building raises again the thought of
how well the old-time builders knew how to win
charming effects. And is it fair to say they did
it instinctively, without definite thought or planning, merely because the average of houses of a
century and more ago was finer in line and
proportion and fancy than the average of to-day?
Rather does it seem more fair and reasonable
to give the old-time builders credit for intending
the effects that they secured. And the immediate application of this lies in the real beauty
and charm with which this up-stairs hall was
planned, with two windows on either side and
with all four deeply recessed; a practically-
planned hall, but at the same time, without
lessening its practical features, a bright and
alluring pausing place.

The deep window-sills are so obviously convenient as places to set things that it is a tempta-

THE UPPER HALL

tion constantly to be resisted; and so there is merely, on one, at the head of the stairs, a line of candles in old brass candlesticks for those setting bedward; on another a great glass Spanish bottle, delightfully squatty and rotund, seen by chance at a railway station, near home, and gathered in by giving in exchange a plain stone jug; on the third sill a bit of Lowestoft; on the last a piece of brass of delectable shape, from the garret of an ancient Norman farmhouse.

CHAPTER VIII

BEDROOMS

A S THE work went on, room by room, it was continually more noticeable with what slight outlay, compared with results, the home was shaping toward an ideal, and continually the feeling with which we entered upon the work grew more strong and certain that it is very much easier to alter a house than to build from the beginning; for how small a matter is a changed partition, a new bit of flooring, an altered door, brass knobs, compared with new girders and beams and roofing and walls and all the money-swallowing outlay of building. To be sure, alterations take both money and time; but not so much as new construction. And with alterations, one may make a home more intimately his own than with building, for with building it would be necessary to have an architect from the very beginning, and the house would infallibly, unavoidably, necessarily, be largely his.

BEDROOMS

It was surprising that there were quite so many changes to make as we found necessary; ordinarily, the home-maker would not find, in a house that was finally to fit his ideas, quite so much that needed altering; but that we did find so much to do, both outside and in, will the better show that any one who loves his home and aims to make it conformable to his ideas can freely alter and transform and successfully meet innumerable obstacles with simple expedients. It is an excellent idea, and worthy of repetition, that luck may be counted upon as one of the resources of the confident home-maker.

When the problem of bedrooms was reached they were found to require as much planning as had gone to the rooms down-stairs.

Light and air are necessarily the first consideration; light and air in plenty; and a plenty that really means a fine and generous amount.

We have not as yet planned for a bedroom out of doors, though that may likely enough come later; always, there is something additional presenting itself to be done. But, after all, a bedroom well windowed can give a very considerable amount of fresh air, and it is possible that, as man has for ages been a being with sheltering needs, has for ages been removed from primitive outdoor life, it may not always be best, in inclement weather as in clement, cold as well as warm, to force himself to bear with rigors; it is possible that there has been a little too much of indiscriminative enthusiasm for out-of-door sleeping, with no regard for the weather or for individual needs. Rooms are a kind of clothing; and clothing, in moderation, is assuredly not always an evil. However, some folk are healthy and sturdy in a sweepingly ventilated bedroom, and others are sturdy who wrap the drapery of their couch about them and go forth to blizzard dreams.

Meanwhile, it is at least reasonable to conclude that indoor bedrooms will always hold their own as being necessary and important.

As we found the house it gave but poor apology for sleeping apartments. The desire had been for number of rooms rather than size and the desire had certainly been carried out. Paraphrasing Lord Bacon a trifle, it may be said that it was a house that had convenient doors and entries but never a fair bedroom.

It was clear enough where the main bedroom

should be: in the west wing, with windows opening toward both dawn and sunset.

There was a small bedroom at the front of the house; there was another small bedroom behind it, opening toward the side; and both rooms were entirely without proper proportion as well as without proper size. These two were to be made one.

When we first saw the house there was still considerable furniture standing in it that the occupant who preceded us had left, although the house had not been lived in for a considerable time; and it was really an aid, in these bedrooms, in showing the limitations. No empty room is so difficult to visualize, as to how it will look when furnished, as is a bedroom, because the necessary furnishings—the bed, the bureau, the dressing table, the chairs—unavoidably occupy so much of the floor; and when we first saw these two bedrooms we saw not only that neither of them had proper space for a bed, either for looks or convenience, but also that neither of them offered the proper position for one. For there are limitations as to where a bed can be put with comfort to the occupier: it must not be right against a window; it ought to be against the middle of a wall; it must be accessible from both sides; and there are adjunctive considerations of light and air and of correlation with the other furniture. And when there is the desirable condition of having twin beds instead of a large single one the problems are a trifle more difficult still.

To take out the partition between the two small rooms was the first thing to do; but this left a bedroom with three doors, and one of the doors led into a short passageway that had suddenly become needless, for it had been built to give direct access from the front bedroom to the back hall, toward the bathroom, and, now that the two bedrooms were one, found its purpose served by the door of what had been the rear bedroom.

Three doors out of one bedroom were not advisable nor was it advisable to maintain this now needless passage. That it took up room was sufficient reason to do away with it, and that its presence made it impossible to give the new-made bedroom proper proportions and arrangement was a still better one. So the passageway was blocked out, part of the space making an alcoved corner by the chimney and the remainder, on the hall side, being made into a linen closet,

which welcome addition to the household conveniences, properly shelved and doored, seems
as if it had always been a part of the house; that
being one of the tests of the success or non-suc-
cess of alteration. A clothes-closet had opened
from the passageway, and its doorway, coming
on the side of the linen-closet space, was lathed
and plastered over; yet, although the closet
was closed in and its door was taken away, it
was neither altered, done away with, nor dimin-
ished in size, for it was only necessary to open
a doorway in its end, instead of in its side; a doorway half the width of the one closed up; and
then to use the original door itself in the new
position, but cut to one-panel width instead of
two.

This bedroom, when structural alterations
were complete, was one of "L" shape, twenty-
two feet by seventeen and a half, the narrowest
of the "L's" measuring eleven feet in width and
the other twelve. An "L" is a very desirable
shape for a bedroom, especially when there is
nowhere a cramped or narrow effect.

With five windows, three at the side and two
at the front, even the most captious could not
well complain of lack of light and air. And

along the base of the grouped three was constructed a window-seat, which, by fitting two parts of the top with hinges, was also to serve, in either end, as a box for shoes. But the carpenter was not permitted, as he desired, to build with lining-boards!

If a suggestion is made to a carpenter to make anything, his mind at once flies to matched and begrooved lining-boards. But it is safe to say that no beautiful thing was ever made of this ugly, belined, much-used and essentially cheap-looking material.

The top of this window-seat is of plain board. The front is made from four panels cut from a door removed from this room in alteration. The shoe-box feature was the merest incidental convenience. The real object of the window-seat was to be something agreeable to look at or from.

Window-seats are almost always attractive, and especially when placed where there is an attractive or interesting outlook; and they have the pleasant usage of centuries behind them, as witness the charming window-seats in the Palazzo Vecchio, looking out over domed and towered Florence, and the fascinating window-seats in ancient castles, facing toward far-reaching views of the Rhine or the Alps and built there by the castle-makers with the purpose of adding to the pleasure of wives who stayed at home and looked out of window in hopes of seeing, along the valley roads or among the trees, the glint and gleam of armor that would tell of the return of husbands from the fighting that was the daily work. The making of window-seats was indeed one of the many delightful things which show that the old-time folk knew a very great deal about making homes attractive, in spite of the absence of what modernists are doubtless right in deeming improvements but which are not all absolutely necessary.

A bedroom should always, if feasible, have a fireplace, even though the room is not dependent upon it for heat. It is so bright and cheerful to sit by an open fire, or to lie in bed and watch one flickering, or to see it gradually dying into a red glow of embers on the hearth as one drops drowsily off into slumber. Myriad thoughts are always aroused by the glow of an open fire: "While I was musing the fire burned," as the Psalmist expresses it.

For a fireplace, fortune was again favorable.

There was, indeed, no fireplace in the room, but in the upper hall, adjoining, there was a flue, with a pipe hole above where the long sofa was to stand, and this hole was closed up, and the chimney was opened for a fireplace in the bedroom on the other side of the wall. The last of our small stock of old mantels, one with fine and dignified lines, was set in place in the bedroom, and over it was placed a long bell-flower garland with knots and pendants. At either end of the mantel was set a brass candle-stick, and in the center a gravely charming little Donatello boy; not one of his laughing ones, for a simpering head is wearying in faïence, fancy, or fact.

That brass andirons were set in the fireplace, following the custom in most of our rooms, may very properly raise the question of whether, in spite of their undeniable beauty, there is not too much trouble involved in keeping so many andirons bright. But, really, the fear of dulling andirons is something of a bugaboo. A thorough polishing twice a year keeps them in admirable condition and appearance; or even if, with time, a patina should gradually gather, why, the patina of age is in itself a lovely thing.

BEDROOMS

An armchair naturally goes with the restfulness of a fireplace; indeed, the desire for an armchair in moments of rest seems inherent in human nature, and one remembers that Major Dalgetty, when a prisoner in Argyle's pitch-dark dungeon, seated himself in a corner, on the stone floor, where he could have a comfortable support on either side, and remarked to Ranald of the Mist that he had always been an admirer of elbow chairs from his youth up.

The color scheme of this room is white: the wall-paper is white, and the woodwork is white, and the color value of the room is dependent upon the white, in combination with the dull black of five chairs, two of them two centuries old, from a New England garret, and with the green and roses of chintz, this chintz being used at all the windows and for the upholstering of the armchair.

For the hangings of a good room it pays to get good chintz. It has a simple sound, and is admirably simple in effect, but if it is of good material, of English make, heavy, and of unfading colors, it is not merely a little flowering calico. Good English chintz is really a work of art, made as it often is from hand blocks, and, although it does not cost so very much over there, it can not be purchased for less than two dollars and a half a yard on this side of the ocean, on account of heavy import duties. But it is not only a thing of beauty, but a thing of beauty forever.

To make the curtains hang well and in good lines, and to obviate the harmful effects of the sun, which is destructive of chintz even when it shines on the back of it, the curtains are lined with curtain lining and interlined with canton flannel. And they are more than ornamental in the room; they are practical as curtains as well, being hung on strong brass rods so that they may slide, when desired, across the window-face. A box-pleated frill on a little rigid wooden cornice, which is also chintz covered, caps and completes each window.

The effectiveness of even good chintz depends upon not having too much of chintziness in a room. It has become not uncommon, especially in England, to have the chintz of the window-hangings repeated in the bed-cover, the uphol-stery of all the chairs, and even in the very wallpaper itself, thus destroying all possibility of good looks by the indiscriminate flood of color.

WHITE WALLS, CHINTZ HANGINGS, AND BLACK CHAIRS

BEDROOMS

That the bed should always be of a generous length would seem to be self-evident; and, in fact, shortness was much more of a fault in times past than it is to-day. More than one of the beds in which Washington slept must have given the wearied general and President poor repose unless he did like Jacob of old and "gathered up his feet into the bed"; he must more than once have thought of what Isaiah, probably under the dire provocation of a sleepless night, bitterly wrote: "For the bed is shorter than that a man can stretch himself in it."

For furniture in this bedroom there was ample space for a great old-time highboy, extremely utilitarian through its ample capacity; facing the highboy is a low chest of drawers, with that swelled front prized of collectors; and besides this there are but the chairs and the dressing table, a mirror in ancient frame, and the pictures—the pictures being very few indeed: one a pastel of a Colonial belle, bepowdered and bepatched, putting on her pearls before the glass of a dressing table precisely like the very one in this room; and no others except two or three water-colors, chosen because of the greenery depicted in them, for this room of white and green and rose. The only rule, again, in pictures, besides the rule of fitness for the particular room (and we have seen a Marie Antoinette going to execution right over the head of a bed!), is that of not showing them with an effect of crowdedness. No matter how admirable your pictures may be, there ought not to be more shown than the walls will properly bear, without that encrusted look that comes from too many good things. An uncrowded look is particularly desirable in a bedroom.

On the floor are rugs: and all of them were definitely made for this room—yet that involved neither the trouble nor the expense that would seem to be implied; for, although they were made to order and of just the desired colors, they were made at very little cost.

This entire question of rugs in a house is throughout an interesting one. To begin with, and speaking broadly, good Oriental rugs (not the glaring ones of aniline) fit any room and go with almost any period of furnishing. With their softly blended colors, they are of any time and all time. Rugs are older than carpets of the tacked-down kind, and an examination of French and English prints and engravings of the 18th Century will show them on many a floor. And if the question of cost be raised it may be replied that carpets also cost, and that although a good Oriental rug of even moderate price costs more by the square yard than does a carpet, yet not so many yards are needed. An old carpet, too, is worthless to the point of scorn, whereas a good old rug may actually increase in value with age. You have known of many a worn-out carpet; but how often have you heard of a worn-out Oriental rug?

However, it may very well be that one does not feel like getting sufficient Oriental rugs for a house of large floor-space, and then comes in the desirability of having other rugs, of the desired colors, made to order—not, as so many architects of to-day think of as the only way, to have Kidderminsters or French rugs extravagantly woven, for in many a room they would not be at all fitting or satisfactory, besides always standing for the extreme of expense— but good old-fashioned rag rugs, braided round ones or woven square-sided, for they are still cheaply made, in New England and Pennsylvania villages, and are of a simple and satisfactory character that goes particularly well in up-stairs rooms and with chintz and white muslin. If one does not care for the trouble of looking up rug weavers and rug braiders, rugs may be purchased at the shops of decorators, in wished-for combinations of color, but they will not seem nearly so much your own, nearly so much the expression of your own choice and taste, as if you deal direct with some old-fashioned worker and discuss with him or her the colors of the plaits or of the warps and woofs.

The doors needed brass knobs and better locks. Fortunately, brass knobs were ready for them; for there is nothing so effective, for so little money, as the changing of the knobs, on doors and cupboards, from crockery, or yellow wood, or weird metal, to knobs of brass or glass or good wrought iron, according to the door and room. Another similar and similarly important point—and it was made a rule throughout all of our alterations, room by room, before the painting—was to take off every one of the cheap-looking little box-like iron locks set visibly on the doors, and replace them with invisible mortise locks.

We find ourselves recurring to the matter of making changes, and securing effectiveness, with slight expense, because most people are persistently and perniciously of the opinion that to gain a good effect much outlay of money must be made. On this point, the experience that an acquaintance had with a high-price decorator stands luminous. The decorator had finished a drawing-room, and, after it was all completed, went into it with the owner for a final survey. He looked at the admirable cornice, the white-pillared fireplace, the chairs and tables, the rugs, the hangings of ribbed velvet reaching to the broad white window-sills. He got up and walked about. He altered the positions of the chairs to a greater informality. He looked carefully over every detail. "There is something else needed," he said quietly; and the owner was quite prepared to hear him order some ormolu, some piece of glorious Sèvres; something, in short, that would be costly, and would come from his own establishment. "There is something else needed—ah, now I see!—you should get half a dozen geraniums, in their plain red flower-pots, and put them on the white window-sills, for the touch of greenery and color and the homelike effect."

Yes; that was a sermon on effectiveness without expense; and as to the ease of alterations, that we persistently stand for, there comes to mind the negative example of a friend who for fourteen years has planned a change which would add daily to his enjoyment. He is independently rich. He still speaks of the alteration as something as ardently desired as when he first spoke of it, fourteen years ago. It could be begun and finished in less than a week and for a total of not over fifty dollars. Yet to him it is still as the unattainable moon to the longing child, just because he cannot put himself in the mood to see how easily things can be done.

There was renewed opportunity to put in practice our theories regarding ease and cheapness of alterations, in the other wing, where, as in the wing already described, we found two small and impossible bedrooms.

The setting back of a partition, so as to increase the front bedroom by the width of a little hallway, was the main thing to be done, thus increasing the size of the front room, but even more important in its results, although less of a thing in itself, was the changing of the entrance door, which was awkward to get to, to a position of easy accessibility. The other room, into which the secret stair from the library emerged, was made into a sewing-room.

The wall-covering in this bedroom was *café-au-lait* color, and, following the design of an old printed fabric, has queer flowery stripes in purple and green. As the wall-paper of this bedroom had both color and flowers in its design, all flowery effect was barred elsewhere, and the plainest of cream-colored striped cotton hangings were used at the windows, thus precisely reversing, in this particular, the scheme of the bedroom in the other wing.

But there was one good bit of coloring, in an old chest, a dower chest, with a wonderful ancient Ginevra-like lock, discovered in a town of the Mennonites; one of those curious sects, migrative here from Europe, who maintain not only their beliefs but their customs, and, keeping apart from what they deem the dangerous world, give a quaintly foreign aspect to those portions of our land where they long ago chose to settle. The chest— and an old chest is always full of suggestive interest—is painted in colors that Time long since gently softened and subdued, but the words of the rudely rhyming motto put upon it by the lover of long ago are still plainly legible, *Lieben und nicht häben ist hartter den Aangraben,* and indicate an unexpected degree of somber ardor, which yet ought not really to arouse surprise, coming from one of a sect devoted to every word of the Book in which they read that jealousy is cruel as the grave.

Old furniture, which, for those who know and love it, adds so much to the pleasure of home-making, and in whose getting there come so many agreeable adventures, ought always by its new possessor to be made as clean and taintless as the newest of the new; an easy task, for with tables and chairs it is only the necessary cleaning and repolishing, while for a chest, a highboy, a sideboard, it merely means interior as well as exterior cleaning, and in every case, for all interior surfaces, after a thorough scrubbing and drying, a coat of common varnish to make everything strictly one's own.

Thoughts of cleanliness come naturally when writing of bedrooms, demanding, as they seem to do, a peculiar degree of care in themselves and their furnishings; and this is remindful that the objection, on the part of some people, to acquiring an old house, is what they fear in possibilities of hidden germs. But there need be

[176]

"AN 'L' IS A VERY DESIRABLE SHAPE FOR A BEDROOM"

no such fears. Such germful and harmful possibilities could be quite done away with: and not only could be, but were, done away with, in every room of this house, up-stairs and down.

Every wall was stripped to the bare plaster, and scraped. Everywhere, nailholes and crevices and cracks were filled with plaster or with plaster-of-paris. Every fault in plaster was repaired. Every floor was scoured, scrubbed, scraped, polished. Each room had all its repairs made before the putting on of paint or wallpaper. And when all these things were done the house was as clean and fresh and germless as a new house fresh from the hands of the builder.

CHAPTER IX

THE GUEST-ROOM

ONE of the stories with which sprightly Mrs. Carlyle was wont to bring smiles to the face of her saturnine Thomas, was that of the Irish burghers who were in difficulties as to the building of a new jail out of the stones of the old one, until the happy solution occurred to them of keeping the prisoners in the old till the new was completed! If the Carlyles had ever altered a house themselves while living in it they would have found a new tang of interest in that story—and even as it was it is possible that Carlyle hardly knew where to betake himself while having builders put into the house in Cheyne Row the inhospitable turning-door that was to permit him to escape from callers. As to ourselves, we really managed, without much trouble, to live in the old rooms while new rooms were being made, making it a convenient reality rather than a jestful absurdity; and for sleeping room, till almost all the rest of the house was completed, used the room that was later to be made the guest-room; it being a room in the old part of the house, directly above the parlor.

In a sense, the pessimist may hold that to undertake the making-over of a house is to undertake interminableness. For the work is never quite finished; there is always something arising that unexpectedly demands or suggests attention. But the optimist may with justice reply that ordinarily the main outlines are well defined and that the end may, practically, be in view from the beginning; and, for our own part, from the beginning we knew that by the time the main bedrooms should be completed, and we should thus be ready to take up the guest-room, we should be nearing the end of the indoor alterations and should be almost ready to begin paying undivided attention to the wide out-of-doors.

Now, by no means all of our expedients, our solvings, our alterations, could be precisely followed by other home-makers. The adventures are not set down with any such thought. But they broadly represent the class of problems to be met by those who attempt the alteration of a house; they broadly represent the character of the solutions and the methods to be followed: and by showing just what our success has been it is hoped to give full encouragement to others to attempt similar home-making. What has been done in this house has been done throughout with moderate means but extreme enthusiasm, and the combination may fairly be deemed to possess potentialities.

The guest-room was a room with a jog in it; a quite unnecessary jog, caused by partitioning off a large part of the room for a stairway to the garret. But even without this there were two stairways to the garret, one in either wing. As we found it, indeed, it was a house of stairwayed complexities. Considering that it had never been anything but a private house, its stairways were positively uncanny in number, there being the three from the second floor to the garret, three from the first floor to the second, and actually four leading up from the cellar! We remember a house, in New York State, that likewise was built with four stairs from the cellars—but in that case we ceased to feel astonished when we learned that the house had been built, some hundred years ago, by the owner of the earliest

American menagerie, and that he had been in the habit of wintering his animals in barns and outbuildings round about and had even kept his tigers in the cellar! Hearing this, we no longer wondered about the four stairs: one for the tigress and three for the egresses, as a local humorist put it:—and we should not have wondered had there been forty times four. But menagerial reasons could not explain the redundancy of stairs in this house of ours on its quiet Pennsylvania hillside, and at length we found that it was from reasons of ménage rather than menagerie. For there drifted to us some small gossip regarding a long-ago owner who, family affection being one of his strong points, had wished to have his son and his son's wife under the same roof with him, but also—both of them being strenuous-minded men, epithetical and maledictory on hasty provocation or even upon no provocation at all—had deemed it best, in the reciprocal interests of fatherly and filial love, to have the two families separated about as completely as if in different houses, thus bringing about an odd combination of association and dissociation.

Stairways had never before presented them-

selves to us as safeguards of domestic peace;
but somehow there was something attractive
in the story of it.   There is such a tendency to
believe that everything in the past was better
than the present—that the grass was greener, the
sky more blue, people more honest, tempers more
equable and less ruffled—that it is highly en-
couraging to find a story perpetuating itself to
the effect that at least some of the people who
have passed away had their full share of quarrel-
someness and of needless irascibility.

To take down the now unnecessary stairway
and the wall that had shut it in was the first
thing to be done, and it gave, in place of a room
with a jog, one widened by more than four feet
into a room of good proportions and good size;
the same size and shape as the parlor immediately below it, and, like the parlor, with two
recessed windows to the southward and two
toward the north.

We have a number of times referred to the
tearing out of partitions as a light task, but perhaps those who have never actually tried it would
like to know more particularly what is the process
followed.

In the first place, there must always be competent knowledge as to the safety of tearing down a partition, competent knowledge as to whether or not it is necessary structurally as a support; and it is generally best to secure the opinion of a builder; it would be extremely reckless to go ahead unless you are competently sure, for although the greater number of ordinary room partitions are readily removable, transferable, destroyable, there are some rooms in which the partitions cannot with safety be touched, in which case the home-maker must plan some different scheme for desired spaciousness; and there are other cases in which, although the partition may be moved, it must not be until another partition has been run up, or beams have been built across, to do the supporting instead. But ordinarily there is no complication or danger in pulling a partition down; and of course it is understood that this is not referring to the outside walls of a building.

The actual demolition may be performed by an ordinary laborer, with crowbar and axe and saw, but he must necessarily be supervised; and the upright studding is worth saving for rebuilding into other work in rooms of the same or lower height. It is really surprising how quickly a partition vanishes—but it is also surprising how quickly the house is filled with the penetrating and pervasive plaster dust! However, the enthusiast does not necessarily notice a thing like that; much depends upon the degree of forwardness of adjoining rooms and upon the immediate cleaning up of the plastery powder, so that it shall not be footstepped through the house.

To repair the floor, if the partition did not merely rest on the floor, is the next thing—and it is fortunate when a rug is to be placed there— and then comes the repairing and plastering of the broken line along the ceiling. This last item may be a trifle more important, as it is wellnigh impossible so to plaster and finish as completely to hide the patch. An architect, himself an enthusiast, was looking over this house, having just been engaged to alter an old house himself. "And I like it better that you have kept that line indicated in the ceiling," he said, in this very room: "I will follow that plan myself and not have everything made to look spick and span new. When it is an old house altered, it looks far better with some indication that it is an old house and not a new one." Well, we do not quite agree with him in this particular instance, but so long as it is impossible to eradicate entirely the sign of a change it is well to make a virtue of necessity.

The character of the guest-room should be that of a room different from other rooms; a different air should be given to it, as something special and appropriate. It sounds very nice to say to a friend that he will be treated "just like one of the family," but that idea, acted upon, would mean carelessness of treatment in a score of ways. A guest, really treated as a guest, can never be just like one of the family, and the very guest-room itself should somehow manage to indicate this. It is realizing an instinctive feeling as old as hospitality itself, a world-old feeling, to realize that a guest-room is not merely a spare bedroom.

But all this does not mean that it should be in the slightest degree stiff, formal, rigid, prim, precise; it should, like every other bedroom, be attractive and comfortable and suggestive of sweet sleep and pleasant awakening. "The Pilgrim they laid in a large upper Chamber, whose window opened toward the Sun rising; the name of the Chamber was Peace, where he slept till break of day; and then he awoke and sang"—

although it has always seemed that a real sense of appreciation of the hospitality that had been accorded him would have made him refrain from this manifestation of joyousness until, at least, he knew that no one of the household was still asleep.

Perhaps some special degree of quaintness and daintiness is an excellent desideratum for a guest-room, but in such a matter one must needs follow largely his own fancy.

The bed for our guest-room is an old four-poster, with its slender Heppelwhite posts topped by a canopy. The posts stand six feet high, and the canopy is therefore at that height at both the head and the foot, but it sweeps upward in the middle in a bow-shaped curve, giving a sense of airy spaciousness. In a sense, every sleeper in a bed is cribbed, but no one wants to be cabin'd, cribb'd, confin'd.

Although, in appearance, the bed is as old-fashioned in every respect as when it was in use in the long ago, in the ancient gambrel-roofed house in whose garret it was found, we made it to accord with modern standards of hygiene and cleanliness by fitting within it an iron bed-frame and spring of precisely the right size, in

THE GUEST-ROOM, WITH ITS DOUBLE OUTLOOK TO NORTH AND SOUTH

place of the original frame of wood. But all this is covered with chintz, reaching to the floor, and the canopy is also chintz-covered: a light chintz, flowered, with parrot tulips. This might sound as if, reversing the Polonian formula, it is gaudy but not rich; but as a matter of fact it is essentially quiet and reserved, for the chintz has much of cream-white background, and although the curtains of the windows are also chintzy, they are only chintz-bordered, the main part being cream-white. One must always be on guard against overdoing chintz.

The woodwork of the room is white, and the wallpaper is a deep green, with a patternless, fabric-like surface. Green wallpaper is one of the things with which one really cannot afford to be economical, as only the best greens will stand the light without fading. In a back hall of this very house we experimented with a very pretty green that was as cheap as it was pretty, and it promptly lost all its color, as is the way with such.

There was a plain little fireplace on the east wall: had there not been one in this room, we should certainly have put one there. But in a guest-room fireplace one must not keep birch logs, or anything else, however attractive, that is not to be burned, for the guest must be faced with a fireplace that offers him the ready possibility of a fire. We remember an old and dear friend, and a most hospitable one, asking, in the guest-room of his home: "Should you like a fire?"—but, although it would really have been welcome, the only possible reply was a "No," so piled up was the fireplace with fans and flummery that would have had to be removed.

In the fireplace, small brass andirons—it was the old custom to have little sets for bedroom use—beside them an old brass kettle full of light firewood (excellent things, picturesque old brass or iron kettles, for such a purpose), and, also beside the fireplace, not only the usual fire-irons but that old-time comfort, needless under modern surroundings, a bed-warmer—which is remindful of the inquiry put to one of us by a fellow visitor to Mount Vernon who, happening to catch sight of one of those old-fashioned domestic conveniences, at once saw visions of a pre-Revolutionary mandolin: "Can you tell me, if you please, what kind of musical instrument that is?"

On the mantel is the usual sparseness, and immediately over the mantel is a pastel, in a plain black frame, of a blue-gowned girl of long ago in the midst of the soft confusion of color of a garden of hollyhocks. There are few other pictures in this room; a pair of mezzotints in oval frames, two old miniatures; and, indeed, one's aim should always be towards not only sparingness in wall furnishing, but quality. When most of the Rembrandts and Corots that are sold are really forgeries, it consoles one to think that it is far better to have a minor original than a major counterfeit. Aim at excellent paintings, watercolors, drawings, pastels, old prints, good etchings and engravings—permit nothing inferior or unfit, whether old or new, and whether the inferiority or unfitness consist in treatment or subject or size. We remember a room which was completely dominated by a painting which overcrowded, overshadowed, tyrannized, oppressed; a painting, good enough in itself, which could have found proper place only in a great gallery.

One of the prolific sources of unfit pictures is friendliness at the season of gifts. "Our pleasant holidays are made whips to scourge us," as it might be quoted—and this applies not alone to pictures but to all the wide variety of household furnishings. As to this, one must from the first make up his mind to be firm. Would you wear an ill-looking hat or gown because a friend or relative gave it?—then why make your room wear anything ill-looking? "Isn't there many another Christmas to pass them along?" demanded Whistler savagely, of a friend who gave the gift excuse for some bits of presented atrocity.

But as to pictures, as with everything, one should follow his own taste only after having tried hard and patiently to make it a taste worth following; and a fresh and tonic breeze of humor comes sweeping in on the subject when one finds Mark Twain's Yankee, a guest at the tower of Merlin, setting down: "It made me homesick to look around over this proud and gaudy but heartless barrenness and remember that in our house in East Hartford, all unpretending as it was, you couldn't go into a room but you would find an insurance-chromo, or at least a three-color God-Bless-Our-Home over the door; and in the parlor we had nine."

This being peculiarly an old-fashioned room, there is naturally a little old china in it—two old bowls for flowers and old blue Staffordshire at the washstand. There is a peculiarly delightful quality in that association with the past which comes from the possession of old china. For it brings up not only bygone generations, with their long-mellowed dignity and stateliness and charm, but it sets before us the people of the past in their most intimately hospitable moments. There is a subtle charm in the touch, as in the look, of old china, in its soft, smooth glossiness of glaze and in the tender dimness of its old-time colors.

If one wishes a guest-room to be really a guest-room, a room for the guest's comfort and convenience, there are some things even more important than furniture, and these are the pins and needles, the quiet-ticking timepiece, the towels, the various things sure to be needed or at least likely to be needed; and with these should go personal care as to sufficiency of heat and light and water. There should be no chance that a visitor is condemned to inconvenience, discomfort, perhaps positive misery, through the absence of personal watchfulness of needs, for it should never be forgotten that a visitor cannot, like a member of the family, so make himself at home as to go about and find or see to things that have been forgotten.

ADVENTURES IN HOME-MAKING

A few rugs are on the floor of our guest-room, and the floor itself, though not of hardwood, is treated and polished as hardwood.

At the first, seeing that the floor was old, of pine, and of boards from eight to ten inches in width, it seemed as if the only thing to do was to cover it with a new floor of hardwood; but the boards were strong and firm, and a first scrubbing, preliminary to occupancy of the room while the alteration of the rest of the house was in progress, brought out—as we knew a waxing would still better bring out—their beautiful natural markings; for, being as wide as they were, they had necessarily been taken from across the very hearts of trees and showed the precious graining. Not only heart of oak may have charm, but heart of pine! And there came to us the memory of floors that we had seen years before, in the houses of a Shaker settlement in Ohio: floors of great, broad boards, in houses of quaintness, cleanliness, peace, houses permeated throughout with the faint perfume of wood fires and beeswax. We remembered that those old Shaker floors, of broad boards marked with heart-of-wood grainings, were polished with beeswax from the Shaker honey house to a glow

[192]

THE GUEST-ROOM

of positive beauty, and we realized that it would be the greatest of mistakes to cover our own broad boards merely because the polished floors of to-day are always made of narrow strips. Stevenson somewhere speaks of the bear's hug of custom squeezing the life out of one's soul, and there was certainly no reason, here, why it should be allowed to squeeze the life out of a room.

But there was much to do besides a picturesque polishing. As with so many good things in this world, the final result was attained only after much of preliminary prosaicalness.

Around the edges of the floor, inheritance from generations of carpet and matting, there was an incredible number of tack- and nail-holes and an unbelievable quantity of tacks still *in situ:* tacks of every imaginable length and kind, single-pointed, double-pointed, hooked, bent, twisted, broken. Every particle of this wreckage had to be removed—an arduous task!—and then every tack-hole, every crack and seam, was made smooth with crack-filler: a putty-like compound readily purchasable, and in whose place putty itself, colored to match the floor, could have been used if necessary.

The floor was at length clean and smooth, but as it was bleached, from the scrubbings of many years, its color was deepened and restored by a coat of linseed oil, brushed on.

Next came the waxing: and that best of proportions was used—a pint to a pound! a pint of turpentine stirred into a pound of melted beeswax; the actual mixing being well away from the fire for the sake of safety. There has been so much poor floor wax sold in this country that it is natural that wax should have fallen into some disrepute. A hard wax is the best, and beeswax is the best of all hard waxes.

Many compounds sold nowadays under the name of beeswax or "mostly beeswax" are almost altogether paraffine. Beeswax is dear, and paraffine is only nine cents a pound at retail, so the temptation to adulteration is ob- vious. Smell is not a good test, for a very little of actual beeswax in a fraudulent composition gives odor. Haven't you noticed that an empty vinegar barrel smells as strong as a whole barrel- ful?

Turpentine is mixed with the beeswax in order to soften it sufficiently to make it adhere easily to the wood; by the time the wax is on, the turpentine has evaporated, leaving the hard beeswax as a coating or skin.

With a room of the size of the guest-room, a pound and a half of beeswax can be used for the first polishing, but after that, to renew the luster, a few ounces for each repolishing will be an abundance.

The beeswax on our floors is applied with woolen cloths and polished with common scrubbing-brushes. There are long-handled brushes weighing twenty-five pounds or so, especially made for wax-polishing, but they are always back-breaking implements, prone to mar baseboards and doors. It was a man out West, a stranger, who, feeling sure we should welcome a good suggestion in the way of home-making, wrote us of his discovery of how easy it is to polish a floor with a dry scrubbing-brush, and since then our heavy, clumsy back-breaker has stood unused. To be sure, brushes wear out rapidly: but they cost only five cents apiece, whereas the heavy implements cost three dollars and a half. And each wax-filled worn-to-the-bone scrubbing-brush ends its career in a blaze of glory as the best of all fire-lighters!

The guest-room floor is not taffy-colored.

And, indeed, why should most people so long have believed that a polished floor must needs be taffy-colored? Oak is not naturally of so yellow a hue; it is more effective when not so highly and artificially toned up. In some of the most carefully schemed new houses of to-day ammonia is used upon the floor, before polishing, to darken the hue of the oak and to avoid the yellow-tawny that has heretofore characterized the American hardwood floor. The guest-room floor is the dark natural color of pinewood age, with its lapse into bleachiness retrieved by its one single touching of linseed oil (a thing not to be repeated!) and its subsequent waxing.

The entire subject of hardwood floors is one of importance throughout, as nowadays every one knows their value as an asset for good looks.

The floor of our principal bedroom we found to be of Georgia pine, indelibly marked, all over it, with the pressure-marks of matting, and two carpenters were employed to plane and scrape it. It cost? Well, something, certainly; but not nearly so much as a new floor would have cost. If it had had a five-sixteenths cover of new hardwood laid over it, that would have had to be scraped and planed after laying, as part of the process.   As it was, the room, a large one, took two men a day, after which it was waxed and polished into beauty.

It was a problem of another sort that was met with in the dining-room.   For that floor had been red-painted, and the paint had soaked in! It was Georgia pine, without a break in it, and all firm and tight around the baseboard.   It was not a floor to destroy or neglect, and lye was used to dislodge the saturative paint.   It took four days; a quarter of the room being treated daily by putting on lye and letting it stand for three hours or so, in which time it ate the paint out.   After each application, it was scraped with a flat steel scraper, and much washing and wiping was necessary to get both lye and paint thoroughly cleaned off.   Here, again, a trifle of coloring was needed, as the floor was rather lye-eaten of hue, and so a very little burnt sienna was applied—just enough to do away with the lye-eaten effect and more especially to destroy any possible lingering touch of pinkiness from the vanished paint.

One thing that our adventures with polished floors taught us, as similar adventures have taught others, is to use beeswax alone, without

ADVENTURES IN HOME-MAKING

any undercoating of shellac, or if, as in one of our rooms, shellac is put on, to be sure and put a coating of wax above it to save the perishable shellac from wear. And, too, there are great differences in shellac, and those with resin in them should be absolutely avoided.

In Europe, the home of the hardwood floor, where it is made and polished to perfection, not only is wax always used as the top surface, but the most general way is to use it without any shellac at all—never, as so often with us, shellac with no wax at all! And what glorious floors they have! what brilliancy and depth of polish! And with what cat-like tenacity of tread one often crosses a palace floor!

But if the American custom of shellacking is followed, it positively needs the protection of wax; without wax, a floor is a constant worry, a prey to the scratching of sand and the scuffling of shoe-soles.

Some do not use wax because they fear it will be sticky—which it will not be if it is proper wax.

Others fear that when their floor begins to look worn and thin they cannot put on another coat of shellac if the floor has been waxed. And, indeed, it is disastrous to put shellac on a waxed surface. If such a floor is to be again shellacked, the wax must first be thoroughly removed. Nor is this hard. Use turpentine to remove it—it being one of the apparent contradictions, that the best thing to get wax on a floor is also the best thing to get it off.

In the restoring of spots or small areas lies one great advantage of wax over bare shellacked surfaces. Wax can be renovated in spots where wear and tear are heavy, and no telltale line will mark the beginning and the ending, but a shellacked surface cannot be touched up with fresh shellac. The entire floor must be done or edges will show.

But why, it may be asked, is beeswax, which is softened by turpentine, any better than paraffine-wax, which is already soft? The reason is, that the paraffine-wax will always remain soft; whereas the turpentine evaporates from the beeswax, leaving it hard and dust-shedding upon the surface of the floor.

A contrivance that is as excellent for dusting up a polished floor as a scrubbing-brush is for waxing it, is a dry ship-mop; a ball or hank, perhaps ten inches in diameter, of cotton string, fastened to the end of a stick. This quite outclasses the usual broom in a cotton-wool bag.

A hardwood floor must not be swept with an ordinary broom. If the floor has a top surface of shellac and is dirty, water and a mild soap will clean it. But if the floor is waxed no water must go on it, for wax and water do not agree. If the floor is just ordinarily dirty, the dry scrubbing-brush will completely restore its polish. But if the waxed surface has sand or dirt ingrained, there is an excellent substance to use, which has only lately begun to be understood here, although in Europe it is a household necessity. This is "steel shavings": soft slivers, altogether of steel, which may be taken in the hand like a handful of wool and used to rub away the inpitted dirt. This steel stuff was imported from Europe for the comparatively few who knew of and appreciated it, but now it is made in our own country and sold by the pound.

One's adventures in home-making should certainly lead him to the hardwood or polished floor, or to the putting of them in if they are not already there. One knows that the poet who sang, "I wish that my room had a floor, I don't care so much for a door," was thinking only of the charm of the floor that is polished.

THE GLASS-FRONTED FIRESIDE CUPBOARD. (See p. 109.)

CHAPTER X

FROM KITCHEN TO GARRET

PLENTY of light and just the right space —those are the primary essentials in regard to a kitchen. Light is such an aid to good cooking that there can be no difference of opinion in theory as to its value, even though there are such very wide differences in practice; indeed, the matter of light was among the very first to be seen to in the kitchen of this house, although it would seem that there ought not to have been shortage of light in any house open on all four sides. And the size of a kitchen is important because there is so much of stepping back and forth, from faucets to dresser, from stove to table, that needless size makes needless weariness and waste of time; yet neither ought it to be small, even though wonders can sometimes be wrought in a kitchen as diminutive as that of a Pullman or of a Harlem flat. There were doubtless times when the easily satisfied old woman who lived in a shoe wished for a little more space.

ADVENTURES IN HOME-MAKING

We had occasion to felicitate ourselves that the home-maker who left us the kitchen left it of an excellent size, seventeen feet by thirteen. And that it was too dark, through there being only one window—the other window, to use a Hibernianism, being a door—was easily remediable.

To gain light, there were two courses possible. One was to open a window on the other side of the room from the window already existent, but this would have looked out upon what was to be a flower garden, and would have destroyed the sense of privacy there. So it was decided to put a window where the door stood. It was, anyhow, one of the numerous supernumerary doors of the house; the kitchen could better be entered from the laundry, immediately behind it, which also had an outside door, very conveniently placed in regard to approach from delivery wagons. The new window added astonishingly to the floor-area of the kitchen without actual y altering the floor area at all!— merely by making it possible to use the space in front of where the door had been. And then came round-eyed admiration of the finished work on the part of the user of the kitchen, with:

"That's suttonly a killing of one bird with two stones!"

There were some things so admirable in this kitchen that, far from being of the kind to be remedied, they were of the kind deserving special praise. We found a broad and generous hearth of brick under and in front of the cooking range: a cheerful, tidy hearth, kept painted with glazed red, and, contrasting with the black iron looming above it, giving a sense of homely cheer and a true esthetic touch!—and it is also a very material safeguard against fire. And we found also a most capacious dresser, reaching from floor to ceiling, with several shelves, enclosed within two doors, above, and cupboards and drawers below, and in the middle a broad open serving-shelf convenient for work: on the whole, a generous, capacious, comfortable sort of dresser, of the kind to be duly honored, revarnished, and appreciated.

The water supply, when we took the house, was from a hydraulic ram—an ingenious mechanism which, working automatically, pumped water from a spring to a great cedar tank in the garret, whence it was piped downstairs and even out to the barn. It was a very satisfactory contrivance, whose maintenance cost only a leather valve now and then, and it just kept on working, without attention. But a ram needs a considerable head of water, as it has to waste from seven to nine times as much as it carries to the tank, and in a droughty mid-summer a spring of even generous size is apt to keep it on short rations, making the house supply somewhat too little for real comfort at the very time of the year when a generous amount is most needed.

Fortunately, the neighborhood began to build up, as we had hoped it would, and, before any very long time after our going there, a big subur-ban water company had laid its pipes to within five hundred feet of the house. This was so much better than the prohibitive two-thirds of a mile that had been the original distance, that arrangements were made to have the water piped for the five hundred feet intervening. All the piping in place for the ram water was ready to use for the new water; all that was necessary was for a plumber to make a connection in the cellar and disconnect from the tank.

The first impulse was now to discard entirely the ram system. It is always a temptation to throw aside, get rid of, whatever has been super-seded. But what to keep and what to discard is often a question. Here, however, it was quickly evident that there was still excellent use for the ram. It was in place, with a great deal of good piping, and so the plumber was directed, when cutting off all connection with the tank, to leave in place a pipe which had always carried the coldest of spring water direct to the kitchen without going to the tank, and so to leave the pipe to the barn as to carry either ram water or water-company water, at will—which, as the company water is all metered, makes a distinct saving. A relief being neces-sary for a ram pipe, and the tank now being a thing of the past, the necessary opening was used to run a fountain in the garden.

At the time of getting in the new water, a further great improvement was realized—the putting in of gas, which, like the water, had approached to within a few hundred feet from the original two-thirds of a mile.

For the value, not only of a gas-range for cooking but of gas-lights in the rooms, as com-pared with lamps and candles, can scarcely be overestimated, especially in connection with a permanent and unlimited supply of water. It makes all the difference between a mere house in the country and a house as convenient as if in the heart of the city. It adds so materially, not only to the comfort but to the actual financial value, for possible selling or renting—and no one knows when occasion may arise to lead him to do one or the other—that there was no hesitation about having these advantages added as soon as it could be done without prohibitive expense, even though we had to bear a good part of the cost of trenching and piping on the highway; for any home-maker should look on such expenditure merely as an addition to the total cost of the house, and as something that more than justifies itself from the most practical standpoints.

An unexpected objection to putting light and water into the house was suggested by a caller, one day: that it is inconsistent with the old-time atmosphere which it has been our object to maintain! As if love for the old could properly mean love for the deficiencies, defects, and discomforts of the old! And as if obvious and necessary conveniences—telephone, furnace, cooking-range, gas, water, facilities for communication and comfort—do not fit naturally with houses of any period! One does not deem it incongruous to go into the city from a Colonial house, by train or trolley. Admiration for Colonial architecture and for charming Colonial furniture does not mean love for Colonial inconveniences, any more than love for an English house, of which there are so many beautiful ones built in America nowadays, means love for English accent, or love for a house of French design means love for French morals.

In spite of our desire to find, in at least some of the rooms, things established just as we wanted them, there was in every room something to be done. This was even the case in the laundry; nor shall we be charged with undue desire for change, or with being altogether too hard to please, when we say that the laundry chimney was the only positively shiftless thing in this entire house—it was a stove-pipe through the roof! ill-looking and dangerous and showing the need of a chimney for the laundry stove.

The floor, too, needed attention, for it was saggingly broken. The laundry is the only part of the house under which the cellars do not extend, and this broken floor required energetic treatment, not only to make it safe and firm, but to keep it from becoming a runway for rats and mice eager to establish themselves in the house—an annoyance that always threatens the country dweller and which it is important to guard against.

The sagging floor was torn up and carried to the firewood pile, and the earth beneath was dug out to a depth of eighteen inches. Noticing that this earth was rich and black, it was conserved for our formal garden.

Small or broken stone was laid to within six inches of the top; on the stone was laid four inches of cinders, well wetted and pounded down; on the cinders two inches of cement: and thus was secured a smooth, safe, durable floor, of an excellent kind for a laundry, and at slight expense—not over ten dollars in all. It has a very slight drainage toward a sewer connection, so that it can be flushed in cleaning.

One section of the cellar also needed a cement floor, all but that one part being already floored with cement, and it was laid for just about twice the cost of the laundry floor, being just about twice the size.

In the cellar there was some coal-bin building

required, but unskilled labor, supervised, readily did this. At a suburban house it is of importance to learn how much can be done without getting specialized assistance; it is a very different matter from that of getting workers in the city. Unskilled labor closed and bricked in a useless window:—there were numerous windows left!—and it was discovered how excellent a shelf the ledge thus made. Under a corner, there were three supporting uprights of wood: but the same worker replaced them with sightly and substantial pillars of brick, putting up one pillar a day. On account of the furnace pipes, a divisional door demanded uncomfortable stooping; whereupon a new door was cut, through which a man can walk upright—a little thing, although it was cut through a great thick stone wall, for it cost, cut and with its sides smoothed up, only five dollars. Such figures are mentioned to show how easily changes can be made, that mean much of convenience, but which most people balk and hesitate about and never get done, on account of indefinite impressions of expense and trouble.

New heating arrangements were clearly needed. Of all the systems, that of hot air has always seemed to us the best, for it brings in a great quantity of fresh air from the outside, a desirable thing in winter, and there is nowhere anything unsightly or space-occupying in connection with it. At the time of arranging for the heating, the water supply was from the ram, whose lack of certainty of water supply barred any thought of a hot-water system; but even without this objection we could not have considered hot water, for its clumps of unlovely pipes must needs stand, winter and summer, in every room, destructive of good looks and covetous of the best spots.

A furnace man was sent for; the kind of furnace we desired being one that we knew of as being very successful in one of the cities of the Great Lakes, where there is really cold weather, for we knew that many of the furnaces in Philadelphia houses were unsuccessful as heat-makers.

The furnace man came and saw and estimated and named his price.

"Well; now give your price on a larger size."

"But this house doesn't need a larger size," he replied.

"Probably not; but it will be surer: and

anyhow, it is always possible to run a small fire in a large furnace—better than to try a big fire in a small one."

And so the larger size was put in. Poor Tom's a-cold altogether too often nowadays, just through a mistaken economy in size of heater, which the dealers themselves abet through eagerness to make low prices to meet competitive bids.

"Aren't you cold in winter?"—such has been the question now and then put to us:—never by an apartment-dweller, although from such an one it would be excusable, living as he does in rooms so closely hemmed in, above, below and on either side, that the wind can scarcely find a window or a bit of wall to blow at. No; the question, when put, has been put by people whose homes occupy hundred-foot lots and are therefore, to all intents, just as isolated as this—the only difference being that here there is the crest of a hill and a thick wind-break protecting from the north wind, and an exceedingly generous furnace in the cellar, besides fireplaces throughout the house. "Aren't you cold in winter?" And what can you say? What is there to say to people to whom a stretch of snow-covered field means only a shudder and who prefer slush and bedraggled sidewalks to the glory of a snowstorm sweeping across a wooded hillside?

One of our rooms came to us—or remained with us—almost by accident; a most delectable room, a room not to do without—for what is home without a workshop?

There are so many things to do oneself, at home, especially when one is a little way from a city!—there are myriads of little things: screens to re-cover, porch chairs to paint, seeds to sort, cold-frames to glaze, upholstering to see to. And there should needs be, therefore, a room outfitted with saw and hammer, with chisel and screw-driver and wrench, with nails and tacks and screws, with miter-box, with paints, lampblack, glue. Why, it is astonishing how often the miter-box alone is used!

The workshop is in a little addition, a sort of one-story lean-to, with a slanting roof, built against the rear of the library wing. The first impulse was to take it down; and then came the saving thought that only a bare, sheer, window-less wall would be left and that it would be far from sightly—and then the further and still more saving thought of not only keeping the room but of making it useful. So it was kept.

And now, as to the garrets. Isn't it Marcus Ordeyne who sets down that it needs temperament for a garret? Why, everybody loves a garret! The very idea of a garret is an idea of romance. And yet the very *raison d'etre* of a garret has always been its advantages as a place of storage, and the charm of the ancient garrets comes essentially from the interest found in the old things long ago stored there—furniture, books, pictures, chests. Every one has felt the charm of a garret, either in his own proper person or at least vicariously through the host of people, in fiction or in fact, whose sensations in an old garret have been given to the world within book covers. Every house ought to have a garret. And if it cannot have old things in it to begin with, remember that what you put in will, a hundred years from now, have all the salt and the savor of age—a sort of attic salt, so to speak.

Sir Walter Scott, warned that the garrets of his beloved Abbotsford would be dark, wrote playfully: "As to the darkness of the garrets, they are intended for the accommodation of traveling geniuses, poets, painters, and so forth, and a little obscurity will refresh their shattered brains." Our own garrets are fortunately so extensive that, leaving the center space, above the pre-Revolutionary part of the house, for the uses of a garret proper, the wings are divided into several comfortable and well-lighted bedrooms. Taking out the great tank, which occupied a room by itself, gave the house another room, and this was made into a third-floor bathroom. It is often overlooked, that a servant needs a bathroom quite as much as does an employer; really more, for a servant's work involves more warmth and dirt. And to have a third-floor bathroom is not only for the sake of the employed, but selfishly, also, for the sake of the household. You cannot demand that a servant be clean unless there be given ample means of cleanliness.

Our garrets are plastered throughout; a great aid toward the general warmth of a house. And it was interesting to notice, on going through an ancient attic in Touraine with American friends who had bought the place, how the old-timers got over the danger of cold air sifting down from the roof; for in that case, the roof being of great slabs of slate, with wind-inviting interstices, sod had been closely laid over every part of the garret floor; sods put with the grass-side down, and now dried and baked with age—seeming, indeed, as old as the time of the builder of the house, Louis the Eleventh, or the man who put improvements upon it, Francis the First. And that Americans of fairly moderate means can go over and buy a Louis-Francis house of beauty —with a garret!—shows what opportunities are still open for delightful experiences in this twentieth century in this workaday world.

Memories of the many garrets we have seen, in Old England and New England, in the Western Reserve, in Virginia, dimly suggest themselves whenever we enter our own dormer-windowed middle attic. And what a mistake there is in the present-day tendency to do away with garrets and make all third floors of strait usefulness alone or at least to make them into billiard-rooms or smoking-rooms or banquet-rooms for guests at social functions—this last use being the least successful of all, for such a third-floor room operates principally to break up all cohesion of parts at a party.

Why, ill-advised or at least ill-advising friends

said to us, warmly: "What a splendid billiard-room you can make this into!" But we wanted a garret. And here, lit by the south-facing dormer windows, are old chests and chairs, old-time prints, candlesticks and snuffers—and it is curious that a pair of these snuffers found in an old house in a shadowed street in Perugia is identically like a pair found in an old house in Central Massachusetts—a spinning-wheel, a three-legged skillet, and ancient odds and ends, such as the great long guard's horn, five feet in length, from an ancient stage-coach—an exceedingly pictorial thing; and, indeed, every old-time print of a stage-coach is careful to show one.

From these old dormers we watched the flying by of the first airship that sailed in view from this house; and while we waited, we saw the lazily moving smoke of a steamer on the far distant Delaware. A century ago, our predecessors probably watched, from these same dormers, the line of smoke on the river that told of the passing of Fitch's steamer (for Philadelphia had Fitch on the Delaware long before New York had Fulton on the Hudson); and we wondered what still more wonderful advance our successors of a century hence shall see.

OVER THE PORTICO: A REMOTE ATTIC FOR BEES

FROM KITCHEN TO GARRET

In a gable—our house lacks but one of being the house of the seven gables—we have just established a colony of bees, and hope for honey and good results; they are over the portico, where no one need go except on bee business, and where there is snug and cozy shelter, with augur holes in a window frame for going out and in. It always seems homey to see bees buzzing about the eaves of an old house, and they naturally take to the old-time garrets, but the special fancy to have bees in an att c has been with us since we used to observe "Uncle Sam," as his neighbors in a little New York town called him, take out his honey from the little garret over his workshop. Whenever asked how much he took out and how much he left in—for the hives must never be stripped—his invariable answer was that he always took out "six dishpans full"; he having taken out just six dishpans full annually for the past fifty years, leaving the bees to wax strong on the rest A few years ago a bee-man, in Ohio, sent one of his assistants to Long Island to establish wished-for bee colonies in the gables of quite a number of the large country houses there. There is a dim old belief in good fortune in bees about the roof.

Bees certainly have peculiar claim to go with things Colonial, for, not indigenous to this country, they appeared with almost the earliest settlers and, as the frightened Indians noted, moved westward precisely as fast as the line of settlement moved.

> "Wheresoe'er they move, before them
> Swarms the stinging fly, the Ahmo,
> Swarms the bee, the honey-maker."

Our first chance—or at least it seemed a chance!—to establish a swarm here, following our long-felt desire, came upon us with suddenness. One day toward the end of June a swarm of bees came whirring with an ominous roar into our garden and buzzed close about a low-set bush. They were emigrants. Where they had come from, how far they had flown, was a mystery, and the only certain thing was that they were bent on making a new home. Not to welcome such immigration would be a sin against opportunity! They had chosen our garden and should be given our gable! Bee-lore was remembered, and a very agitated black boy was set at beating a big tin pan with a potato-masher, and meanwhile the carriage sheet was stripped off and spread upon the ground about the shrub. Fortunately the tradition that they do not sting when swarming met with no painful disillusionment; and that they settled upon the bush, winding themselves about it in a thick and enormous coil, seemed to prove the correctness of the tradition that pan-pounding causes them to settle, although bee experts disapprove of anything so noisy. At any rate, the pan was pounded and the bees did settle down. Hurrying to the telephone, a bee-hive was ordered, for immediate use, the bee-man, three miles away, being told that an emigrating colony were on a bush, and that we were about to gather them up in a sheet. "You don't need to do that," he said. "They will stay right on that bush and I will send the hive right down." Why, why, did we follow his advice! Why did we not remember to beware of the man who knows!—Well, the tin pan ceased from troubling for the bees seemed well at rest. And then all at once, before the hive arrived, they quietly slipped off and left us beeless. They chose an unwatched moment; some scout had returned with tidings; and we knew that from their bourne the bee travelers would not return.

Well, the hive came—and before long we

filled it in a more prosaic way, by purchase rather than by bee chase; and bees became occupants of their secluded part of the garret.

It is a highly excellent quality of a real garret that its positive demands are so few. It does not absolutely require that much be in it or that much care be given it. Even the airy cobweb does not demand the broom. A woody smell, a bunch of herbs, hanging from the roof alongside of sunflowers for the chickens, an easy old chair beside a dormer window, the light filtering through swaying maple leaves, a book of verses underneath the bough—an ancient attic's paradise enow.

CHAPTER XI

A SECLUDED PORCH AND FORMAL GARDEN

IT WAS with positive joy, it was with zestful relish, that we turned formally to out-of-doors; we loved every part of our home, but, after all, it was out-of-doors that we had come to the country for, and we wanted more of it than could be seen from the windows. And, too, as to interior work, no matter how pleasant in itself or how satisfactory it seemed to be in results, there had to come a time when the constant dust and plaster of it demanded a change.

We were to find, out-of-doors, as we had found indoors, that with small expense, but with enthusiasm, any one can win delightful results. Wealth is not required nor is unlimited leisure. As with the house itself, we were to find it a matter of faith and works; and we were also to find, as with the house, that one must begin by getting his facts from his imagination.

We first took up a part of outdoors that was almost indoors; the rear porch; so built, as it was, between the two wings—they reaching back farther than the middle of the house—as from the first to give an impression of seclusion. We aimed to make the seclusion still more apparent by the making of a formal garden. And what was done and how it was done is told for the same reason that led to the telling of the adventures with the inside of the house:— to show how easily results can be attained.

Now, whether the desire for a secluded porch was the cause of the formal garden or the desire for a formal garden was the cause of the porch, is not perhaps entirely clear. Somehow, there came the idea of the two as not only juxtapository but mutually supplementary, and the more we thought of it the more it seemed an idea worth carrying out. In a sense, of course, the porch was the beginning, for a porch was there when we took the house; but it was not a porch that was at all ready to be treated as a livable adjunct; it was not, to begin with, part of what might be termed an outdoors decorative scheme.

The house, with its slope of hill rising grad- ually behind and another slope falling charm-

ingly away in front, is itself, with its lawn, on
practically level ground; and yet, although almost level, there is sufficient rise to set the front
door three steps above the grass while the rear
of the house is on a level with the land.

The rear porch was on a level with the floor
of the hall—we had fortunately found and put
in place the long glass doors to connect the two
—and we planned to have a formal garden on a
level with the porch; or, to be precise, just six
inches lower than the floor of the porch.

The original porch floor was of wood, but
was not at all in usable condition. A porch
floor of wood, on any house, is the part first to
show dilapidation. Under the low-set floor a
great deal of the rain drainage of the hillside
had got into the way of washing freely in, not
only to the damp detriment of the cellar but to
the damp demoralization of the porch flooring
itself, though efforts had been made to preserve
this flooring by an air-space beneath.

The obvious remedy, for permanency and
for good looks, was a porch flooring of brick,
and the natural impulse was to fill beneath it
with stone. Luckily, however, it was suggested
to us that the stone would act as a dry ditch

and form a direct water-course to the cellar!—
which it assuredly would have done. So instead
of a base of broken stone, there was filled in a
base of thick red clay, the kind that cuts like
cheese and yields to no man's shovel, thoroughly
tamped into position. On top of this clay was
put a layer of finely crushed stone, and on top
of that a layer of cinders, and the immediate
bed for the brick was of bar-sand.

Now, all this sounds elaborate and trouble-
some, but in reality it was work that was easily
and cheaply done; much of the material, such
as the clay and the broken stone, was found on
the place, and the cinders and sand were dumped
just where needed. Fear of the difficulty of
such work ought never to hinder one from proper
safeguarding. It becomes a delight to know that
even the things not seen are of proper quality,
depth, material; and this is one of the pleasant
advantages of having things done through your
own initiative and in your own way, by laborers
under your own direction, rather than having
work done by contract.

The buying of sand, at least in this part of
the country, shows the home-builder that he
has a thing or two to learn, for the ordering of

[224]

a couple of tons or so would seem to mean enough to scatter over a big space, whereas, the legitimate but rather droll custom being to weigh sand wet (very different from sugar!), a ton can nearly find accommodation in a barrel!

The brick were easily and rapidly laid in two days by a good bricklayer. We had ourselves chosen them, for their color and hardness, at a brickyard, two miles distant, as there are great differences in brick. They were laid in squares, thirteen inches on a side, with a black brick-bat in the middle of each red square—this being our time to learn that a brick-bat, a "bat," is not a brick, as we had supposed, but, in bricklayer's parlance, a half-brick. The bricks (it took only thirteen hundred) were laid on their sides, instead of on edge, and thus only about half as many bricks were needed, while the effect was quite as good.

All this was sufficient to give permanency and attractiveness of flooring, and reasonable provision against dampness, but an additional bit of work seemed advisable as additional precaution;—this being the building of a concrete retaining curb extending down three feet in the ground, any possible danger from water being so serious a matter that we were ready to do works of supererogation for the salvation of the cellar.

The brick-paved porch, with its glass communicating doors and with windows looking intimately out upon it, making it really a part of the house;—the garden, beginning at the very edge of the porch and seeming to grow out of it and be part of it;—each a complement of the other—both together uniting to form one scheme —that was the plan.

Nor was the garden to be large. The porch was thirty-two feet by ten; the garden was to be of the same width, thirty-two feet, and only twenty-five feet in depth. All of the porch and much of the garden were limited on the sides by the wings of the house, and for the rest of the space the garden was to be stone-walled. The entire impression wished for was one of simplicity, intimacy, unpretentiousness, seclusion. Great size was not needed, nor was great expense. And the sense of seclusion was much increased by a background of nearby retinosporas and firs, that were delightfully dusky and environing without really keeping the sun from the garden.

THE SECLUDED PORCH AND FORMAL GARDEN

A SECLUDED PORCH

There was no garden there to begin with nor had there ever been a garden; worse than that, there was no soil for a garden, for the owner from whom we bought the place had commenced some changes of grade, and had had the top-soil of our garden spot all scraped away, leaving nothing but terrible yellow under-soil, worse than worthless for garden purposes. His intent had been like ours so far as cellar dryness was concerned, but as a garden was no part of his plan the soil had been carried a half-mile away, and was not at hand ready to throw back as a top layer after the digging-out should be completed. Our own first work was to have digging and grading continued; for the digging had to be deeper than the intended level of the formal garden, to leave space for putting in necessary garden soil.

This matter of soil is not understood by all of those who go out to live in the country. It is only by experience that one learns—as we did in a garden of honeymoon days by planting perennials in a bed of gray clay thrown out from a new cistern,—that sub-soil is sterile with a sterility that seems impossible to subdue. It is only the upper layer of the ground that is good for growth: for the growth of things desirable, that is, as weeds seem to have the unhappy faculty of growing anywhere! The upper layer of earth is rich with decayed vegetable matter and with various deposits containing elements chemically needed for plants. But get below this dark layer of humus, and—with clay even to a greater degree than with sand—there is a barrenness of soil which is positively hopeless. Elementary though this may seem, it is only within rather recent years that general attention has been paid to it. It used to be that when a house was built, the earth from the cellar and foundations was spread over the good soil, around the house, spoiling that soil by submersion, and making an area where plants or grass would be for years ungrowable. Nowadays, in building a house in the country, all the top-soil, where the house is to stand, is first cleared away, and conserved to spread later over the newly graded land.

The digging out of our garden, and the filling in with garden-mold, woods-earth, compost and general richness, with somewhat of sand to neutralize the heaviness of the clay, involved considerable work, but no one who loves a garden ever begrudges work upon it, and before planting is the time to be thorough. It raises a pleasant picture of the past, to think of the elder Pitt, the great Chatham, forgetting the cares of state and the bitter contests in Parliament, the stress of war with France or with America, and working with such loving eagerness upon his garden as even to have relays of laborers digging and delving by torchlight.

It will be noticed that making a garden is not, as is generally supposed, merely the planting of flowers. We had the entire garden built, as a matter of construction, before we thought of planting a single seed. And as a result—although this is anticipating—the garden, completed, looks thoroughly well even in winter, with its permanent squares, its walks, its walls, its box-borders, its sun-dial. The Italians, famous garden-builders that they were (were, more than are!) showed how to treat gardens as essentially a part of architecture.

The retaining-wall bounding the farther side of the garden and part of one end is of unusual width—two and a half feet—and tha is for both looks and usefulness. It is but two feet in height, above the ground, but three feet below—five feet in all. There was plenty of stone, of a delightfully weathered color, from a nearby crumbling wall, once a divisional wall, that needed to be done away with.

It is surprising, how the general effect of seclusion in the garden is increased by this retaining-wall, only two feet above the ground as it is; not a single inch above the level of earth behind it, but with grass growing on a level with its top, thus making it what the English, with no thought of the humorous, call a "haw-haw" wall.

The wall was laid dry; without mortar; and the depth of three feet was more than safety from heaving by frost required; but it was meant to catch all rush or seepage of water that might come from the hillside above, and to keep it from the garden, and it does this successfully, carrying the entire flow to one end, so that it goes off at the farther end of the house. For such rainwater as naturally falls in the garden, there was underdraining put in, with the continued intent to do even the unnecessary rather than have risk of a damp house.

The garden itself is to be walked in or sat

beside, but has in no sense regular thorough-
fares, and therefore its ways are ways of pleas-
antness and all its paths are grass. A three-
foot width all round its edges was sodded, and
three-foot paths were laid out across it from the
middle of each side, thus crossing each other in
the exact center.

There are thus four small flower beds:
square-cornered except at the corners toward the
middle, where they are rounded to frame a
circle. And in the centre of the circle, giving
the garden an old-time atmosphere of quiet
restfulness, is a sun-dial.

The sun-dial pedestal is an ideal sun-dial
pedestal in size and shape and character; eight-
sided, with capital and base, and mossy-gray
in color; yet it was only a discarded, old-time
earthenware chimney-pot, cast aside long ago
in the deep grass beside the house, and seized
upon, when found, as the desired pedestal.
That is one of the principal assets for successful homemaking—the cultivation of a sort
of extra sense for the seeing of what is usable
and where to use it. Dickens, you remember,
saw the pedestal for his sun-dial in a bit of bal-
ustrading of the old bridge that they were de-

stroying at Rochester, and he proudly seized upon it for use at Gad's Hill.

So fortunate a find was our chimney-pot and so admirably did it suit that we gave much attention to mounting it properly. It stands on a foundation of well-sunk concrete, on top of which it was firmly squeezed down within a small-sized cheese-box, as a mold, filled with cement, leaving, when the mold was removed, a visible base seven inches high, below the pedestal, two feet high, upon which the slate sun-dial was screwed. A party of surveyors, who chanced to be marking the boundaries of a neighboring field, courteously fixed the exact north for the gnomon of the dial, thus making all complete. So well does it mark the hours that all the household have grown accustomed to cast an eye at it to see if luncheon is late.

One day, a most faithful adherent of sundial time asked: "What do you suppose dey cos'?"

We had not bought the sun-dial; it had come by gift; but we ventured: "Oh, five or ten dollars, perhaps."

Two big eyes grew rounder and bigger: "Lawdy! It takes less'n that to buy a clawk!"

A SECLUDED PORCH

The garden was for old-fashioned flowers; and to begin with, nothing is more old-fashioned than box. (Think of iconoclastic Queen Anne ruthlessly destroying the glories of box at Hampton Court! They are lamenting it yet in England.) So each bed was outlined, around its edge, with slips of box from a broad and ancient hedge standing in never-to-be-explained isolation, far from the house. Box is reputed to be not only among the most difficult of shrubs to move, but even to propagate by slipping, and so we went at the task with care. Slips about six inches long, whittled, on one side only, to a point, were gathered from the big hedge and set close about the flower beds, each slip being planted in a handful of sand. This was in March; and the slips were patiently and persistently watered for thirty days. The result was even better than we had dared to hope, and for those slips that died we waited until the following March to fill in with new in their places.

It was interesting, the other day, turning over the pages that tell of one of the most lovable characters in all fiction, that Bishop Myriel who befriended Jean Valjean, to be reminded that his garden was divided into four box-bordered squares by paths and that another path ran all around the edge. But the Bishop's garden was three parts vegetables to one part flowers, and when told one day, by Madame Magliore, in a sort of gentle mischief, that he would be more consistent if he had it all in vegetables, and that lettuce is more useful than blooms, he only replied that the beautiful is as useful as the useful!—even more so, perhaps, as he added pensively.

Throughout, this is distinctively an old-fashioned garden. Each bed, inside of the deep and glossy greenness of the box, is lined with the massed blossoms of sweet-williams; in the center of each bed were planted bulbs of the superb Madonna lily, although thus far these have largely remained an unrealized ideal; and, besides these, "the Flowers are divers in Stature, in Quality, and Color, and Smell, and Virtue," for the path-bordered squares glow with the wonderful blue of delphiniums, the white and pink of fox-gloves, the wistful beauty of pinks and pansies, the yellowish bronze of coreopsis, the pure white of Canterbury bells, the fragile beauty of Shirley poppies. In each bed, the planting was relatively similar, and the choice was such as to have flowers in bloom through spring and summer and fall.

The middle of the retaining-wall was slightly recessed, opposite the sun-dial, and in the recess was placed a lion's head ten inches high, of iron, seen one day on a nail in the dusky shop of a Florentine key-maker in a narrow street leading to Santa Croce; a grizzled, stooping, queer old man he was, who looked up blinkingly from his forge and, seeing American eyes bent upon that lion's head, firmly demanded one lira—only twenty cents for it! In the lion's mouth was a hole that was clearly meant for the spouting of water, and then and there it was resolved that somewhere and some time, in America, it should be put to its proper use. "I got it from an old garden," said the old man quietly. It is set in the middle of the recess, and below it, flat against the wall, is a rondel of pink marble, eleven inches across, in appearance very much such as one sees on Italian walls —but which was actually found in a corner of our own attic, being apparently the discarded top of a small stand of quite modern times. It is precisely the thing to set off the Italian lion's head, from which the water comes tricklingly down over it into a little basin beneath, formed behind a curving doorstep of stone.

But before water ran from the lion's mouth we had an experience. When the earth was dug out for the foundation of the wall, it seemed the best time to lay the pipe, from a hydrant outside the kitchen, to where the lion's head was to be. Gradually, in the course of clearing up about the place, pipe had accumulated, and a fine fifteen-foot length was chosen as the main piece for the purpose, and so it, with shorter pieces, was jointed and laid in the ditch and the solid wall built above. Later, connections were made and the water turned on—but only vain splutterings and hisses ensued. And it was found that the long piece of pipe, our *piece de resistance*, had a long split in it and that we had actually paid a plumber to have it taken out of the cellar, some time before, and a sound length put in its place. Well, such things add to the gayety of households—and at the same time teach humility. And controlled but sardonic was the glee of the plumber, when he found that he was to be, a second time, paid for replacing that same length of pipe.

A SECLUDED PORCH

We first came to have affection for the secluded porch when we used it, in the early days of our adventures, for the storage of sorry-looking mahogany doors and chaos of embryotic paneling material, which we liked to go and gloat over, picturing their future use, and to contemplation of which we were at times so ill-advised as to lead our much-loved but grinning friends. Well, doors and panels are a tale that is told, and here we are in our transformed porch, brick-paved beside its garden. And we love to breakfast in its quiet shelter on hot summer mornings.

The pillars needed some disfiguring scroll-work removed, and the porch ceiling, with its visible beams—which had never been painted, but only oiled—was given a couple of coats of spar-varnish and thus changed in color to a splendid warm brown. At one corner is the cold-air intake for the furnace, and this rectangular opening in the brick, up against the wall, was grated with bars of three-quarter inch wrought iron, obtained from the blacksmith and built solidly in place by the floor-layer; looking much better and being much stronger than the usual cast-iron grating, and costing scarcely anything.

But alas! one day down fell a little duckling between the bars, only to be haplessly followed by all five of his brothers and sisters, who Indian-filed downward after him. The bars were immovable; they were too close together for an arm to reach through: and the little ducks quacked their consternation in dismal unison, while various futile attempts were made to relieve them. But at length it was remembered that in the garret had been seen a corn-popper, a memento of some previous owner, and it was found to be just the thing to pop the grateful duck ings out of their dilemma.

Looking into the garden are numerous windows, but best of all is one from the workshop; for it is a dear, delightful, delectable window; a smallish window with thirty-two small panes. But it was not always there, naturally though it now fits into its environment. We saw it, one day, in passing, as the sole window of a temporary tool-house, a flimsy little cabin, put up during some construction work. The foreman was spoken to. "Do you care to keep that window after you have finished here and torn down the toolhouse?" "No." And for one dollar the window was brought to our home.

A SECLUDED PORCH

Over and over again, as has already been remarked, luck may be counted as one of the assets of the enthusiastic home-maker. Have need of a thing and it wil show itself. Only, one must learn to recognize a thing when he sees it.

We wanted two long settees, for the ends of this porch, and were on the watch for them. Then, one day, they began to tear down, for remodeling, an old lyceum building in a suburban town three miles away. Driving by, as the work was in progress, we looked in. It was an interesting old building, in which many a well-known lecturer of the past generation had held forth for his literal hour on the stage, and tradition told particularly of Emerson. They were discarding the old seats—they were long benches—and we were made cordially and freely welcome to any we wanted. It was the psychological moment. Decision was to be made at once, without preliminary home measurements, and we picked out three—two for this porch and one to set at the front of the house under the library windows. They were carted home, and were found to fit in with the architecture of the house to a peculiar degree; we have never seen other settees just like these; and they are far better-looking, of better shape and proportions, for this house, than any other shape that we have ever come across. They are narrow and high, with an odd suggestion of a curve to the back, and very, very comfortable. That they were talked to by Emerson adds materially to their charm; and there was something most fortuitous about their length. We had expected them to need fitting—but the one for the front of the house was precisely as long as it ought to be; one, for the secluded porch, was of the required dimensions, to an inch, to reach across the end; and even the third required only such alteration as half an hour of work by household hands could give it.

CHAPTER XII

THE LAWN, THE SHRUBS, AND THE TREES

LORD BACON, with his intense devotion to literature, law, philosophy, science and statecraft, was assuredly a fairly busy man, and yet, in spite of this wide and absorbing variety of occupation, he also found time to devote himself to the pleasures of growing things out-of-doors. And he sets down the very wise dictum—he being a very wise man—that "nothing is more pleasant to the eye than green grass kept finely shorn." Well, all England is proud of her shorn green grass, and her damp climate is a great aid toward growth and greenness, and here and there are bits of lawn that are splendidly good, as that at Warwick, which is perhaps the very finest in the entire kingdom; and could ancient Warwick the King-Maker have laid claim to it he would doubtless have rejoiced in the appellation of Warwick the Lawn-Maker.

Naturally, when we ourselves turned our thoughts to out-of-doors, we wanted a lawn.

16   [241]

But to begin with there was really nothing of the sort. "There was no lawn out in front of the house in the place where the lawn ought to grow." There was an agglomeration of shrubs. In fact, all that front space might fairly have been described as being infested with shrubs. And that they were really fine shrubs did not seem to make any material difference. It was a striking example of the right things in the wrong place.

A quarter of a century or so before our advent, a lover of trees and shrubs, one who not only loved but knew them, had planted here. He had put in a really splendid variety, including dark English yews, flaming Pyrus japonicas, retinosporas, dogwoods, yellow-glowing forsythias, giant magnolias, deutzias, Virginia fringe-bushes, mock oranges, lilacs, Pride of Rochesters. They had been short and slim; now they were sturdy and broad: at first, it was a case of shrubs scattered over the lawn; in course of time it had become a case of grass appearing among the shrubs. It was an object lesson on the evils of promiscuous planting.

As between shrub and lawn it need never be a case of loving one less and the other more.

[242]

THE LAWN, CROWDED WITH SHRUBS, AND AS IT APPEARED
AFTER THE TRANSPLANTING

LAWN, SHRUBS, AND TREES

They should balance and complement each other. Shrubs should not speckle a lawn. They should border it, bound it, give it definiteness of outline. And as shrubs make a background for the lawn, and a lawn should merge into the shrubs, so trees should be a background for shrubs and the shrubs should merge into the trees.

It is worth while to study this sort of thing, for it means so very, very much for the good looks or bad looks of a place. And when you have done your best to balance positions and size and foliage and shapes and colors—when you have planned your work and worked your plan and made yourself as much of a landscape gardener as fate and fortune will, it is well to remember that Wordsworth, wrapped up though he was with thoughts of the importance of his own art, deemed this kind of work, when done excellently, to be in the same class with poetry and painting.

To transplant the wrongly placed shrubs was what clearly needed to be done; for we felt strongly averse to killing them and clearing them away. It is always a pity to kill a shrub or tree that has been growing for years—and it is so easy a thing to do as actually to seem almost ignoble. It is well to remember that Washington's fame does not rest upon his cutting down a cherry tree.

Yet there are times when a tree or a shrub must either be cut down or transplanted; and when it would be too unpromising or too expensive to transplant, the only alternative is thus to cut down. And here, right in front of the front door, were two arbor-vitæs that had been allowed to grow to scraggly misshapenness and were too large to attempt to transplant unless with regular tree-movers and apparatus, and so the ax was laid to their roots, to use the Biblical phrase. It is rather odd, by the way, that although the Bible and Shakespeare have a great deal to say about planting and watering and growing and cutting down, they are silent on the matter of transplanting, or, at least, we can remember no such reference. With both, a tree is a fixed condition, and it either lives or dies where it is fixed. Even when Birnam Wood was to go to Dunsinane, the huge promise of the beginning tailed off into the extremely tame makeshift of carrying a few lopped-off branches!

Almost all of our wrongly placed shrubs, fine

large bushes that they were, were transplanted to spots where they were needed.

Transplanting shrubs is not easy. It is not a matter of going out and changing a half-dozen before breakfast, although most people think it is until experience teaches them differently. We rather thought so ourselves—but our first transplanting undeceived us. It was in May—a month when no shrub ought to be transplanted—and the beginning was made with a couple of hydrangeas. Looking back at it, it seems as if the process was not so very far from being like that of an impatient man who moves a boy by grasping him by the shoulders, dragging him from his seat, and setting him down violently at another spot. Not, however, that we felt at all impatient with the shrubs. We merely had the right way to learn. And fortunately for the shrubs and ourselves we saw the importance of learning.

But if we did not from the very first have transplanting properly done, it was not from lack of advice. The trouble was, the advice was what Sam Weller would have called "warious." In regard to one of the English yews, a friend told us that the extremely large ones in front of

Columbia University Library—twice the size of ours—were merely carried there by three or four Italian laborers and set in their holes without any preliminary care and without any ball of earth around their roots. "I was a Columbia freshman at the time and remember watching them. So you see how easy it is to move a yew." But another said: "I know you remember those fine yews on the terrace in front of the library out at Columbia. Well, I knew the landscape architect who moved those yews, and he told me what a trouble they were, and that he had forty men and a regular moving-machine, and carried a six-ton ball of earth on each root. Those yews never knew they were moved."

No doubt it is true enough that in a multitude of counselors there is wisdom—but the difficult thing is to find just which one of them has the wisdom!

We did no more transplanting until winter-time, having soon learned that that was the best possible time; better than the fall or spring; and our winter movings were so successful that the shrubs lived and throve. In winter-time, shrubs feel least the shock of change, and it is the best season for carrying a large ball of earth on the roots, for it will freeze there—although it is not necessary to aim at six tons! But for good large shrubs, of say from twenty to twenty-five years old, the ball of earth should run well up into the hundreds in weight: say at least from five hundred to a thousand pounds, the only check being inability to move it.

First dig a trench around the shrub, from two to three feet deep. If this work is done in September and filled in temporarily, fibrous roots will grow around the immediate base of the shrub and strengthen the shrub for transplanting. If you err, err on the side of depth; a fine shrub will outlast your lifetime and should not be begrudged an extra hour.

The earth-ball, around the roots, should be at least from three to five feet in diameter.

The new hole should be dug before the moving is begun, and it should be lined with straw to keep the sides and bottom from freezing. It should be considerably larger than the root-ball, for there should be room to put quite a quantity of mold in. The new hole should be wider at the bottom than the top, thus giving opportunity for the roots to develop laterally in soft earth and to seize a vigorous hold.

We are presuming that the actual moving is not done by men whose business is moving, and who have special machines, with levers and slings, and great wheels between which the shrub is low-hung for cartage, but that it is done with the strength and skill of amateurs and amateur assistants, and with the amateur's ropes and packing and his sledge or stone-boat.

Before beginning, reduce the size of the shrub one-third. It must necessarily be trimmed back in this way, to balance the unavoidable cutting-away of much of the roots, and it is better to trim before moving rather than when in final place, because it makes easier the trench-digging and then the actual handling of the shrub —especially if it be a prickly one! And it is also better to tie up the branches before moving, as it greatly simplifies the work and largely obviates danger of breakage. Ropes are liable to cut: for ourselves, we put the family trunk-straps to this unwonted use. And we used burlap or old horse-blankets freely, throughout the moving, to shelter the roots from drying wind, and to avert breaking and barking, keeping in mind again that in aiming at a result that is to last for years a little extra care should not be withheld.

To handle our big shrubs, long beams were used, with a leverage of ten or twelve feet, and with these, aided by spade work, the shrub was gradually pried loose and pushed up heavy sloping boards to the edge of the trench, where an improvised sledge was ready.

Or the ball of earth, with its enclosed roots, was gradually raised from the hole by slightly tipping from side to side and filling under at each tipping. The shrub was thus kept in practically a vertical position until the bottom of the root-ball was on a level with the sledge.

It is important not to lift out hurriedly. Impatience is destructive. Better move one well than half a dozen destructively. The temptation is to drag loose before sufficient earth has been dug out. The non-professional is apt to tear and pull and thus to cause damage or ruin.

It is really best to freeze the ball before moving, for ease and safety in carrying, and some expert movers pour water over it to form a coat of ice, although others prefer merely to let the earth freeze naturally. Actual freezing is not absolutely necessary, but a day that is wet or cloudy should by all means be chosen. If it is unavoidable to take a dry day the root-ball should be carefully covered with burlap, and the hole into which it is to be set should be thoroughly soaked. It is well, in a dry season, to soak the hole for a couple of days or so.

Extreme care in shielding and covering the roots during removal is requisite on account of the imminent danger of shriveling and killing the roothairs or the feeding-cells by exposure. A few minutes of exposure to drying air may be sufficiently disastrous to kill the tree or shrub, especially if it be a conifer.

When the shrub is planted in its new hole, the earth, the rich loam that is to be put about it, must be heedfully packed in. This is not a difficult matter when the root is frozen within a ball, though even then it must be done with care. But when the tree is transplanted without a frozen ball the packing is a matter of high and delicate concern. The fingers must be freely used if the best results are to be obtained, and the earth must be thoroughly manipulated into place with the "infinite capacity for taking pains" which is the basis of successful transplanting. There must be no yielding to the notion that throwing in mold with the spade is "just as good."

Accompanying the finger-work there should be careful and repeated shakings to settle the earth into unreachable interstices, and then comes the final ramming and packing.

The actual moving of each shrub was not much of a task; it was just a matter of moving the sledge, on wooden rollers, to the new location, and then sliding the shrub in—the rollers being the tops of some cedar grape-trellis posts that had been taken out because of rotting around the bottom. Horse power was first tried, but it seems as if a horse must be trained to such work, for it only jerked strongly and unexpectedly and broke the harness!

When all else is done, the shrub must be helped through times of drouth, not only throughout the first summer following the planting but even perhaps the second and third summers, or a sad and wilted specimen will result.

Once in a while we asked ourselves if the final result was sufficient to make up for all the time and care; and the only possible answer was yes; for we had thus secured big shrubs, generous in size, well established in places where they were needed. To have bought little shrubs of a nurseryman, would have been far from as satisfactory, and to have bought big shrubs, like these, would have been expensive or impossible; and shrubs from the nurseryman would themselves have entailed a great deal of labor and watching and watering. And there was still another reason. With shrubs taken from one part of your own place to another, personally seen to by yourself in every detail, there comes an addition to that intimate personal possession that is in itself so pleasant.

When a shrub was removed, there was always an unsightly hole to fill; and these many holes were made disposal places for a great deal of broken glass and crockery, tin cans and rusty iron, found littered about the place. Such stuff was filled into each hole to within a few inches of the top, and then good rich earth was thrown in and carefully tamped and packed.

Flower-beds, like shrubs, are usually disfigurements when on a lawn, and one of chrysanthemums and one of peonies that we found here had, like the shrubs, to be moved. There was no place ready for the chrysanthemums, and

THE FINISHED EFFECT IN FRONT OF THE FINISHED HOUSE

so (it was May that was chosen, and it is a good month for these flowers), they were separated and set out in the vegetable garden, and by the ensuing year had, in the good old phrase, multiplied exceedingly. The peonies were a root-bound mass, tight knotted together. They were taken out in October, before the coming of frost, that being the proper time for handling them. Peonies send up their shoots so early in the spring that spring-time transplanting is very dangerous for them; indeed, they are not likely to survive a spring experiment.

The peony, the Chinese emblem of power, possesses a spirit of gentle obstinacy and must needs be humored! Should you desire to lighten up a dullish corner with its splendid glow it will not give you obedience; it will set forth nothing but green leaves, without the flowering stalk. Only in bright places will it display its beauty, and so, yield gracefully to its caprice, and plant it beside a sunny path or along a sunny embankment, away from the shadow of wall or shrub or tree. We set these out bordering a path leading away from the library door, and they grew delightfully there.

At one side of the lawn was a fountain: an

admirable thing in itself, but this had a fat Victorian boy, in pink and green, perched on a pedestal and tight-clutching a big fish in shades of blue! Yet it would have been foolish to condemn the fountain on account of shortcomings of Victorian art, and so the boy and the fish and pedestal were removed (afterwards making glad the heart of an itinerant junkman), leaving a low-set fountain alone. The basin needed digging out preparatory to cementing it and repairing the wall, and an Italian—"a gooda digger"; we had his own word for it—was set to work. It was all carefully explained, partly in his own language, partly in our own, and partly in the universal language of signs; and as it was a simple job there seemed no possible difficulty. But the Italian was even simpler than the job. With him, digging had always been moving on in a straight line—and when, in an hour, he was again looked after, he was indeed proving that he was a good digger, for he had dug straight out, through the brick wall of the basin and into the lawn, and was headed with busy pick and shovel in the general direction of sunny Italy.

Our general plan for the lawn was simple.

LAWN, SHRUBS, AND TREES

For quite a stretch directly in front of the house, the ground had only a slight slope: then came a short sharp dip, and the trees and shrubs that were in place there were to be left. In front of the west wing all trees and shrubs were to remain, just where they were, for they began, there, with some tall retinosporas, perfectly placed just at the turn of the drive in front of the house.

The taking-away of shrubs, to make a clear stretch of grass to the dip of land, made an open space in front of three tall firs—splendid Nordmanns, branched to the ground—and left them to form the immediate background of the lawn. When fronted by the massed miscellany of shrubs they had appeared quite insignificant, and indeed quite unnoticeable, but now they were in a position to be seen in their beauty of form and color.

Even the most loyal American cannot well endeavor to have only shrubs indigenous to America, for so many of those most common or most beautiful came originally from other countries; the lilac from Persia, the forsythia from China and named from a Scotch gardener— but even a partial list would be surprisingly long. One pleasant feature of early Colonial life was the interchange of plants of all kinds between America and England, and not a ship crossed the ocean, from either side, without sundry packages of seeds, sundry bulbs, sundry plants and trees. A favorite way was to ship young trees in hogsheads. England profited by flowers and shrubs and trees from the new land of America, and America profited by those from settled England. And if, nowadays, we get some from Japan and China it is really but a continuance of the profitable intercourse between continents.

The dogwood, however, is indigenous American, and is one of the two or three most admirable, having peculiar charm in spring from its glorious white blossoms, in the fall from the glow of its red berries and the bronze-red of its turning leaves, throughout the entire season because of its foliage lying in charming stratified masses, and during the entire year because of its general shape;—an irregularity of shape, and attractive, as irregularity so often is, like the crooked smile of a Barrie heroine. When, coming to the place, we found a row of large dogwoods bordering the fence of the pasture, we felt that no discovery could be more charming.

Well cleared of superfluous shrubs, and put into the desired final shape, the lawn was now to be made of proper finished appearance. A landscape gardener would have advised ploughing over the entire space, leveling it, and planting it anew. But we did what, under the circumstances, was better and at the same time far less costly, as grass seed for a large space is a large item in addition to all the cost of ploughing, grading, and rolling to prepare the surface. To remedy little heights and depressions, lawn surgery was practised—cutting across the uneven places, laying back the flaps of sod, and filling in or taking out as required, and then laying the sod back again. The entire lawn had once been a good and properly graded one, and the grass still in place was excellent. It would have been a needless pity to spoil what was there. So all the big bare spots left by the filled-up holes of the migrated shrubs were planted thick with grass seed. In two seasons the entire lawn came into good and level condition, and in all the expenditure of at least one hundred dollars was saved. A definite objection to ploughing, too, was that there were a number of stumps, just under the surface; not only those of the two arbor vitæs, but quite a number from long-previous decimations. A fine lawn always requires a great deal of care to secure it and a great deal of care to maintain it in condition and appearance, but there is nothing that more satisfactorily repays care.

Shortly before our taking the place, there had been a general looking over of the trees, and quite a number had been chopped down, on account of hopeless injuries by lightning or for being for some reason or other in the way; for even excellent trees may crowd each other too closely. There must have been twenty great gnarled stumps and roots—for the roots had been grubbed out most systematically—lying here and there, and we had them carefully hauled and rolled to the wood-yard for conservation as fuel. But it was found to be labor lost, for ax and saw and even wedges made no impression that was commensurate with the efforts made. So there was another hauling and rolling out into the vegetable garden, and the gnarled stumps were piled together, and there was a great fire lasting for two days, and the result was not only the disappearance of the undesirable stumps but the leaving of a great mass of fine wood ashes, one of the best of fertilizers, which was then spread over the lawn.

Two or three of the largest—to go back a little—it had been impossible to move, and so dynamiting was resolved upon. The dynamite was bought several miles away, and it was on the drive home with it, that, passing an old gentleman, a slight acquaintance and almost a neighbor, he called out cheerily and suggested that he get in. An inquisitive old gentleman, he: and before long he turned the talk with hints of inquiry as to what could have caused that particular drive so early in the morning.

"I merely wanted to get some dynamite, and so—"

"Dynamite!" His face grew white and he gasped.

"Yes; and so—"

"And have you g-g-got it with you?"

"It's under the seat. It's packed in with—"

But he did not wait to be told how carefully it was packed. Never, surely, did so old a man get out of a runabout with more agility. Safely on the sidewalk, but intent on securing and maintaining a still greater distance between us, he yet did not wish to appear rude, and rather quaveringly called out, as he struck a rapid gait back in the direction from which he had come, the obviously true statement that he "just wanted to get out here!"

A man accustomed to handling dynamite bored and filled and calmly tamped the dynamite in. But the dynamite labored and did not bring forth splintered chunks: it was far from blowing the stumps to bits: and so they, like the others, were made into wood-ashes fertilizer.

Our predecessor had done admirably in cutting down trees that overcrowded and overhung. For our own part, we have such keen distaste to cutting down a big tree as might perhaps have made us permit even undesirables to remain.

Quite a proportion of the trees still standing —there are over a hundred on the place—are evergreen, of one kind or another. Nor, contrary to a somewhat general belief, is there anything mournful or funereal about them. On the contrary, their being green in winter as well as in summer tends toward the opposite of mournfulness. That, contrasted with other trees, they are dark, does not mean that they are mournful. And for a wind-break—for which purpose a long line of hemlock-spruce stand behind this house, toward the north— the evergreen is the only kind worth while, as the other trees have but bare branches at the time when a thick shield is most needed. And a really beautiful feature of evergreens is their annual putting out of tender green growth at the end of every branch and twig, giving each tree a most fair and fresh appearance.

One not only comes to a personal love for his trees, but by living with them learns to differentiate their various sounds, especially in the quiet of a night when they stir and sigh and murmur and rustle in a gentle breeze. There is the frou-frou of the maple; there is the long and swishing sigh of the willow; there are the soft voices of the evergreen; and even when all is so still that all other trees are silent, there is the vague whisper of the fir: and they are restful sounds, those voices of the night.

"Old shade," as country folk call it, is one of the greatest assets of a house. In buying, one should be ready, if necessary, to pay a much larger price for a well-shaded place than for one that is bare. And this would seem self-evident were it not for the many bare and shadeless houses that one sees. One of the grimmest things in history was the reply made by the governor of St. Helena when told that Napoleon complained of the absence of shade at Longwood. The Englishman, in words suggestive of interminable time, sternly replied: "Then we shall plant trees."

Close in front of our own house, on the land between house and driveway, are two matched and towering maples. But we found them rather irregular in looks, and there were places where a little decay had set in. In fact, the trees were not at all well.

When you are sick you call in the doctor. When your horse is sick you call in the horse doctor. Then why not, when your tree is sick, call in the tree doctor? Tree ailments, like human ailments, are doctored largely with the knife. The tree doctor is not only a tree doctor but a tree surgeon who performs many an operation. And after you have watched him clean and fill cavities you will think him a dentist, too.

Send for a tree doctor, and he will come with extensive paraphernalia—with ladders and ropes, with saws little and big, saws short-handled and saws with handles so long that a man may stand on the ground and reach far up into the branches; he will come also with knives, with chisels, with clippers, with tin, with healing and protective unguents.

There was a beginning of decay here and there where a limb had been broken by wind or lightning; here and there was a cavity to clean and fill; here and there was a surface to cover thick with tarry paint; there were bumps and shoulders from evil lopping of the past. No inexperienced hands could have done what that tree doctor did with those great trees. And how nobly the trees responded to the care!

By watching a tree-doctor at work, and by talking with him, one comes to a better understanding of trees in general and of their ailments. From him you may learn many an interesting fact. He will tell you, for example, that the ancient idea that the heart of the tree is the most important part is a superstition. "The tree was decayed in its very heart!" is an old form of expressing what was supposed to be the worst possible condition. Yet it is not the heart that is vital. The heart is important, in common with the rest of the trunk or branch, as supporting wood. When too much supporting wood decays the tree falls. But the vital, growing energy is immediately beneath the bark, and a tree may live on with its heart eaten out so long as enough wood remains to support it. And it is fortunate for the sake of history and legend that this is so. What would history do without such trees as the Hartford oak that hid the Charter, and the hollow tree that sheltered Charles the Second! What would legend do without such ancient shells as Robin Hood's Larder!

CHAPTER XIII

THE SPRING-HOUSE AND STONE-WALLED POOL

WHY it is that Nature does so much to make trouble for him who would live in the country is a puzzle as ancient as the first garden. Why it is that weeds grow faster than flowers, why the rag-weed flourishes through a drought that kills the bean, why the wire-grass revels under discouragements fatal to the tomato, why insects swarm on flowers and vegetables but never attack the dandelion—why, indeed, pernicious insects flourish at all, and why moles and field-mice gain a generous living on such precious provender as lily bulbs and tender peach trees, is all a mystery, unless one is willing to set it all down as part of that general system of the universe under which evil flourishes more easily than good and at the expense of the good. Burns writes sentimentally of such depredations and says that the country dweller will "get a blessin' wi' the lave, and never miss 't"; but, after all, he was a poet who, after unsuccessfully trying to farm, made his living as an exciseman!

But there are times when even the most pessimistic must admit that good things flourish as luxuriantly as the proverbial green bay tree, and such a time is when he looks at the things he has planted beside a pool: for a pool so soaks into the land round about, so seeps and percolates, as to make whatever is set out grow generously. At the same time, the very serious danger must be avoided of letting the ground near by become a soggy bog, which was the result attained by one of the characters in Humphry Clinker, who put a pool in the middle of his field and found that the whole field became a swamp. But with the pool on our place, sogginess of the surrounding earth was easily and entirely obviated through its being in a sort of natural depression, with the ground higher than itself on three sides and with thorough precautions in regard to drainage on the fourth.

One single gleam from the water that Nature has turned into that pool, one single shimmering up through the greenery of the sloping hillside, is enough to make one forget any infliction of

THE BARN, AS IT WAS

THE SPRINGHOUSE AND POOL, AS THEY WERE

weeds or insects or field-mice or moles. And Nature so generously, so opulently, so prodigally, so freely, always offers her splendid aid to the homemaker! Not only does she give the glimmer of water and lushness of growth, the charm of trees and the sweet glory of flowers, but as adjuncts to the looks of every house she offers the blue of the sky as the noblest of backgrounds, she offers the green grass as the most marvelous of carpeting, she offers the tender quivering play of lights and shadows as the most precious adornment. If one comes to a love of Nature, and even the slightest appreciation of how she strives to assist him to make his home beautiful, he can never again complain seriously of pettinesses.

A characteristic of Pennsylvania is the springhouse; it is one of the things that every old-time house expects to have; and our own house was no exception, for we found the ancient springhouse still in place, nestled above a spring of great volume. A little, low, stonewalled building it was, with one of its thick walls rived but not burst by a decades-past stroke of lightning that had freakishly sought out this lowly building, and with its old beams blackened by the resultant fire. Yet it is not in the least the trembling and superannuated structure that such an introduction might be expected to portend, but is still sturdy and strong, under its roof of huge, hand-made shingles, mossed by age.

Inside, there was much of messiness, and the reservoir pool had to be deepened and broadened and a concrete curb put in to raise the level of the water, for at first it was to be our sole water supply, with ram and tank, till we could make arrangements to connect with the pipes of a water company as soon as they approached within possible distance of the house. Whitewash was put on with unsparing hand—it is astonishing what a renovating agent whitewash is, in such places as cellar or barn or springhouse!—and for the general sake of appearances two barrelfuls of white pebbles were scattered over the bottom of the pool. "But that is useless!" we were told. "They will all sink in the mud!" However, they were sprinkled in, and fortunately they all lie there in sight, making a white, clean-looking bottom.

The springhouse possessed, rather supererogatorily as it seemed, a little and small-windowed loft, which has proved to be a handy place for the storage of porch chairs and various odds and ends. But on the whole the loft is little used except as a playhouse and nesting-place of a few "chipaneezes"—a word used in all good faith, and which would scarcely be thought of as intended to represent "chipmunks"— which points out that for puzzles philological one need not feel compelled to roam so far as to Max Muller and Sanscrit, as there is always something interesting near home.

There had once been a pool, catching and holding the water from the spring, about twenty-five feet away from the springhouse, and it had even been enclosed with stone, but all we found was a wet and stagnant spot, with tumbled-in remains of wall, most of which had been carried off for some other use. A tradition came to us that the pool had once been actually full of water, but that it had been so for only a short time, because pond lilies had been put in, and "pond lilies always draw muskrats," and that the muskrats had dug such holes as to carry off the water and cause general discouragement.

We were not without genial suggestion in regard to what to do, as the springhouse and potential pool aroused a good deal of friendly interest.

"I'd fill all that in," said one.

"I'd dig it deeper and make it a swimming pool," said another.

On the whole it seemed best to have the pool just for the allurement of its being a pool and to let all the swimming be done by picturesque water fowl.

"But you'll know lots more about water before you get through with it," was a final warning, coupled with some remarks concerning the eccentric and unaccountable ways of water and the exceedingly strong probability that this pool—should we ever succeed in making it a pool!—would either run dry again or become green with scum.

Rough stone was hauled there and the walls once more built up, the three sides where the land rose a little higher than the level of the pool being built without either cement or mortar. The earth backing these walls being a thick clay, we felt that nothing more was needed, and the result justified that impression. But with the fourth side there was considerable difficulty, and several times, after the pool had actually filled, the water all escaped again, and in the end we found that a thickness of concrete must be run up on the inside surface of that entire side. However, home talent was sufficient to set the concrete, and it was easily done, and since then there has been no difficulty. The bottom of the pool is the clay naturally there. The water has never shown even an indication of scumminess, and this is probably because it is constantly entering from the springhouse inlet and leaving by the outlet pipe built in the end wall.

The pool is fifty-two feet by twenty-seven, the size being controlled by the contour of the land, and it is surprising how much of life and color and animation is given by a piece of water of such a size.

Below the pool, the drainage is altogether underground, except that it is made to emerge for a drinking basin in the pasture, after which it is again carried underground, making the pasture one broad sweep of land, for the unbroken growth of grass, instead of having it broken by the rough and irregular bed of a little stream. This work had been done at much expense by our predecessor and adds distinct value to the field as either a pasture or meadow. The water does not come out into view again till among a grove of trees a quarter of a mile away—and this is remindful of an experience with water-cress!

We wanted to grow water-cress, and remembered a man who had the hobby of shaking in water-cress seed, wherever he came upon running water, and especially at sources, on his walks around the country, thus bidding fair to stock his entire county with the plant. And in many places it came up, to his own delight and presumably that of others. Well, we were not so altruistic as he, but at least would scatter seed at our own source and have it grow in our own water. So it was scattered— but no plants came! And only by chance did we discover that it had all floated underground, and had grown up by the stream-side in those woods! Not to be thus circumvented, however, we gathered a number of mossy stones to which the growing cress was clinging and carried them to the pool and set them in. But even thus, victory was not ours, for it so chanced that, water-cress being a dainty tidbit for ducks, our ducks promptly devoured it all; being con-

siderate enough, however, to leave the moss.
After that we gave up water-cress.

We found mint growing by the pool, so freely
as to make the entire vicinity aromatic; indeed,
the odor might be termed intoxicating, even
without the familiar bibulous concomitant.

Within the pool itself tall cattails have sprung
up but their natural lush growth has been so
checked as to keep them at one side and mainly
in one corner.

Outside the pool, around the edge, it was only
natural to set iris, for the water and the gray
stones of the wall made an ideal setting for the
purple flowers and the blue-green lance-like
leaves.   This was set out around three sides in a
natural-looking border, without formality, while
the side farthest from the windows of the house
was planted as a thick foliage-bank of graceful
forsythia and elderberries, nothing being more
cool and refreshing than the white panicles of the
elderflower swaying above the edge of the water
in midsummer, and nothing being more charming than the delicate yellow shafts of the forsythia
in the earliest spring.   Ferns, too, are around
the pool, and columbines, with their bursts of
white, and in the grass are daffodils—the be-

loved daffydowndillies of Spenser—and everywhere the bank is dotted in summer with the
red of the English field poppy, a red that is at
the same time flaunting and reserved.

The pool is shaded by great willows, with
long pendants dipping down toward the water,
and by mulberry-trees and the Magnolia glauca.
Close by stands a monster old cherry, that in
spring is a metallic gleam through all its branches
from the myriad of tiny black cherries that mass
upon it—cherries not to be picked without
infinite toil but which clothe the tree as if in
myriad shining links of chain armor. Above the
springhouse itself and the little channel that
connects it with the pool stand thick-shading
butternuts, chestnuts, and locusts.

Through that narrow, stone-bordered channel runs the water to the pool, and almost at
the pool edge the water passes into a little cir-
cular basin, stone-enclosed, made by setting
there a big discarded iron basin from the fountain at the side of the lawn. Ugly there, it is
precisely what is needed here. Not a sign of
iron shows, the bottom of the basin being covered
with sand and the edges having been covered
by carefully laid stone.

An Italian—but not the good digger!—put the basin in place and also set in, as the bottom of the short outlet to the pool, a great long narrow stone. Italians, and especially those from Italian country districts, are likely to be particularly clever at this sort of work, when they understand just what you want done, as even the simplest peasant is deftly familiar with building and handling stone; but they know little of the action of our frosts. There is great likelihood, in putting in such a basin as this, midway in a channel of running water, that the water will dip under the edge of the basin instead of flowing into it.

Crawfish are great enemies of any stone-walled pool, by digging persistently at interstices till a leak is made, and quite a number of crawfish were dwellers here, which would have boded ill had not the ducks soon found them out and treated them as they had treated the water-cress.

Ducks ought to be a successful race; they know so positively just what they want and they so positively set themselves to get it. Amusing they are, too, as they swim and race and dive. You see a group paddling, with the oddly graceful hands-behind motion, when suddenly one stops and in an instant has her head plunged under water. She hurls herself like a javelin at some bit of food, and in an instant her tail stands perpendicularly in the air and her feet are wildly waving. Down goes a companion head, and then another and another. There is a group of twinkling tails and waving feet. Then one duck resumes her natural position and paddles off, another follows and another and another. And then there floats by a stately white China goose—"floats double, goose and shadow," as Wordsworth might have put it; and anyhow, one suspects that his swan was really a goose, for on the water one looks as well as the other, although "swan" sounds more poetical.

With a few ducks and geese one comes to a realizing sense of the admirable meaning of some of our words, such as "ducky" and "goosey," for nothing is so particularly "goosey" as a goose, except when it is on the water, and nothing is so "ducky" as the cute and yellow baby balls of duck fluffiness, and nothing is so preposterously ugly as the rare "ugly duck-ling" with its weirdly ridiculous motions and its big, bare, googling eyes.

PRESENT APPEARANCE OF SPRINGHOUSE AND STONE-WALLED POOL.

SPRINGHOUSE AND POOL

We have a whimsical friend at the pool, too; whimsical acquaintance, rather, for thus far he has rather maintained his distance and has not concluded to accept such slight advances as have been made. A tortoise, he, a land tortoise; and although he keeps up a residence near the water it is apparently only for the sake of the scenery, without any idea of going in— although he did tumble in, one day, and was discovered clinging to the rocky side in a decidedly uncomfortable position, from which he was doubtless glad to be relieved although he only went away with his usual indifferent, shuffling fumble of a walk. We found a date, 1902, cut into his back, although there is no way of telling how old he was at that time. White of Selborne had a tortoise that was at least thirty years old, and knew of one that had attained at least a century of age, so in all probability there is still plenty of time for this tortoise and ourselves to get acquainted.

CHAPTER XIV

THE SELF-SUPPORTING FEATURES OF A COUNTRY HOME

AMONG the very keenest of all delights is that of eating the peas and potatoes, the peaches and pears, that grow on one's own place. It is not merely the fact that they represent economy; indeed, that is but a very small part of it. For the sense of pleasure has in it an essence of the ethereal: there is something in the fact that things have grown for you, on your own place, that gives them a sort of magic flavor, not to be understood by him who has never experienced it. And on this place we have reveled in abundance and variety.

Not that it is a self-supporting home. It is far from being that. To make a place in the country self-supporting is a business all by itself, demanding skill, patience, application, unlimited time. In fact, many a home deemed self-supporting would not be thought so if value of property and interest on investment were figured. And in any case, it would demand that a place be given up primarily to farming, whereas with us the farming features were to be quite incidental. It would demand that one's lifework be the work of his crops, his fowls, his stock, and that they be given all his thought.

Yet this place has so many self-supporting features as to add tremendously to the general satisfaction of country living and to decrease materially the living expenses. One of Smollett's characters took over a farm that yielded a revenue of one hundred and fifty pounds a year, but, making it into a country home, he found that, so far from still giving a revenue, it cost two hundred pounds a year to keep it in condition. But that was too much on the order of the farming of that well-known New Yorker who, when a guest at his country home asked for a drink, responded: "Shall it be milk or champagne? For one costs as much as the other!"—which ought not to have been the case. Every one, with ordinary care and common sense, and with paying a fair degree of attention to his place, ought to find its incidental yield very profitable. Sir Walter Scott sets down, somewhere, that from his Abbotsford estate, to which he did not look for revenue but only for mental and physical advantages, he received sufficient produce to save him nearly a thousand dollars a year on what he should otherwise have had to buy. But perhaps that goes too far in the other direction for a man who is not a professional agriculturist; after all, Scott was a great fiction writer, filled with poetical fancies!—It reminds one of dear old Herrick's poetical boasts of his country home, and of how he got twenty bushels of returns for every bushel sown and how his teeming hen did lay her egg each day—which it certainly did not, his poetical fervor causing him to forget the off days.

The average good hen lays about one hundred and fifty eggs in a year; some individual hens going considerably over that and others under. But the matter of laying, even in the warm months, is to quite an extent a matter of chance. One hen may lay a great deal of the time, while a sister, of the same brood, may simply not lay at all. Being feminine, it is a matter of "if she will, she will, you may depend on't; and if she won't she won't; so there's an end on't"—

except that one must be ready to go further and promptly make a salad-end of the offender. But although one cannot make a hen lay, she can be encouraged, and the best encourager is proper food. A hen needs what is called a "balanced ration." At all times of the year she needs both vegetable and animal food; at all times of the year she must have some kind of green stuff. Feed such things as meat scrap, chopped bone, skim milk, whole wheat. Daily, in very cold weather, it is well to give a hot mash of some such foods as bran and vegetables and chicken peppers; corn, too, is excellent as a warming food. But ordinarily let the hens keep busy out in a big chicken yard, picking up not only the food you have scatteringly fed, but also the multitudinous and infinitesimal titbits that they tirelessly peck for. That terrible word "henpeck" comes from the hen's terrible, tireless, nervous, incessant, unceasing work.

The original chicken-house was on low ground near the pool; it spoiled the looks of the pool, and in fall and winter would surely make the chickens rheumatic, so it was cleared away and the chickens domiciled in what had been the cow-barn, their quarters being prepared by taking out stanchions and feeding-troughs and wooden floor, and making a big, roomy, sunny, stone-walled room. It is wind-proof and cold-proof when doors and windows are closed, and at the same time gives ample opportunity for sun and air, with inch-mesh protective screens across all ventilating openings.

It seemed best to have a floor of good clay upon a foundation of broken stone, with a wall of concrete around all the edges to a depth of eighteen inches below the surface, to prevent rats from tunneling in. In theory, rats are efficaciously kept out by a stone wall, but as a matter of fact intelligent and indefatigable rats make little of tunneling through mortared inter-stices. After all, they have little to occupy their time, and perhaps accept a stone-wall challenge as an ennui-destroyer.

The roosts are not of the kind that mount up, bar above bar, like a broad step-ladder. Those are a survival of the days when chicken-houses were not made "varmint-proof." It is better to have parallel bars of one height, be-cause upon them the hens do not crowd and push and fight for the highest perch. The bars should be low, about two feet from the ground, so that all the hens can fly up easily, and they should be square-edged because claws clutch square edges better than round ones. They should not be nailed fast, but held in place by long nails, loose, like pins, in round holes. The whole thing should come apart quickly and easily for cleaning and whitewashing in the sunshine. Whitewash, with carbolic in it, and an occasional spraying with kerosene, put the finish to any mites, crawlers, or germs on the roosts. Care may kill a cat, if the old proverb is true, but it will save your hens. Chickens do die so easily—one of the facts to which the persistent optimist shuts his eyes. There are hawks, owls, crows, possums, weasels, minks, foxes, rats and cats—pole and plain.

To see several hundred pounds of your home-raised chickens walking about on the hoof is vastly pleasant. There walked the roast of yesterday; there struts the o'er-confident to-morrow; and you count innumerable eggs before they are laid. Who that knows what a fresh morning egg tastes like can return to a shop-worn product! How can a family that has learned to distinguish a pullet egg from an old hen's egg by taste return to even a guaranteed dairy-shop breakfast! How can the housewife, used to an egg basket always full, be content with a dozen of the aged from a store! How can a household used to chicken and cream gravy, to a small pair roasted, to the charms of frying size, broiling size, roasting size—even the stewing kind and even the chicken-salad sort, fresh, wholesome, clean-fed, clean-housed—how can such a household ever again be content with cold-storage poultry, even if a benign government should stamp an assurance on the tail feathers that it is not over six months dead! Why, it almost makes one lyrical.

Every one in the country ought to have, must have, will insist on having, a vegetable garden; but the mistake he will probably make will be having it too large and thus increasing the labor of it. It is surprising how small a garden can be, and still give produce with ample sufficiency. For our own part, we started with one quite too large, and cut it down greatly for the ensuing season, putting clover for winter chicken rations in the unused part. Intensive gardening is the thing.

Cauliflowers, tomatoes, peas, string beans,

lima beans, cabbages, corn, beets, carrots, potatoes, sweet potatoes, celery, spinach, peppers, okra, parsnips, asparagus, rhubarb, squash, cucumbers, onions, endive, lettuce, parsley, canteloupes, egg-plants—we find it easy to grow all these, and they come to the table with the inimitable flavor of absolute freshness and the fine quality that comes from good seeds. We specialized on two or three things—cauliflowers, early and late, and peas, beginning the peas with the earliest possible days and, by successive plantings, a row at a time, getting a supply far into the autumn. And this successional planting gives great results with other vegetables as well.

It used to be that there was a certain time for planting each vegetable. Once given its planting that vegetable was finished for the season. There was a time for beans and a time for peas, a time for rhubarb and a time for corn. Now it is known that planting may be done for a long succession of maturings. You may almost, as Marcos Bozzaris might have exclaimed, plant till the last warm day expires. The art of succession is the art of success.

With some vegetables the matter of succession

takes care of itself. A single planting of tomatoes will furnish a continuity of blossoms and
fruit till heavy frost comes.

We were at first inclined to feel dubious in
regard to the garden soil, it being a heavy clay
rendered cloddy by a well-intentioned but mistaken deep ploughing in a wet November. But
after a season it recovered and we learned that
although it was not so good for some things it
was better for others. And it reconciled us
very much to learn that a wealthy man, living
four miles away, had made a liberal offer to
our predecessor to buy the entire top-soil of
the garden, which he would have had hauled
to his own place for the sake of growing asparagus, as he knew of the former asparagus results
here. The offer, fortunately, was not accepted,
and we found that the soil was indeed remark-
able for growing the succulent asparagus.

And, even for other vegetables, the soil needed
only breaking up and lightening with sand, and,
of course, constant fertilizing.

Fertilizers should never be neglected. They
pay, not only in ampleness of return, but
quality. And if you keep only one horse and
one cow there will have to be more or less ferti-

lizer purchased in some form or other. Plants are thirsty, and need water. They are hungry, and need food. Fertilizers are food for them. And it is of importance to find just what food the different plants need and then to find just what fertilizers contain those foods, the requirements being various.

The principal plant-foods are three: nitrogen, phosphoric acid, and potash. Some fertilizers contain all of these constituents, in varying proportions; some contain only two; some but one.

One should buy, therefore, the kind he specifically needs, instead of merely ordering, as is usually done, "a bag of fertilizer." The laws of almost all the States demand that the constituents of each fertilizer be plainly marked on each bag. And these bags of fertilizers are not inexpensive trifles—possibly on account of some such fact as that imparted by Mark Twain, that "the guano is a fine bird, but great care is necessary in rearing it."

Among the very pleasantest and most valuable self-supporting features is that of fruit, and in that respect we were very fortunate. Delicious cherries, a variety of grapes, Concord, Niagaras,

Salems, fine apples, a tree of fine Bartlett pears—such things came to us with the place. But we at once began to think of the future, as well as the present, and not only pruned and trimmed but set out numerous young fruit-trees, especially peaches, they being quite short-lived and requiring constant reinforcement.

The grapes were given a particularly thorough pruning, and, when tied in place on new wire and posts, responded munificently. They, even more than most fruits, require highly skilful pruning, and, fortunately knowing this, an old fruit-grower was engaged to come and do it. Cut wrongly, grapes will be ruined for years. Beating spears into pruners is all very well, but from the standpoint of a fruit-grower there are times when one is tempted to think that pruners do the greater harm.

As a warning not to trust too implicitly even to a man who knows things, comes an experience with a line of apple-trees. We found them to be suffering from the dreadful scourge of San José scale, and the old man who so successfully pruned the grapevines declared that every one of the infested trees must be cut down and burned.

[288]

THE CHANGES AROUND THE BACK DOOR (See ch. xvi.)

There was no doubt that it was really the San José. There was the scurfy deposit, grayish in color and a trifle rough, and when it was scraped it showed a yellow liquid, from the killing of the scale-lice.

The ways of the San José scale, which has devastated so many thousands of orchards, are curious. The full-grown scale is about one-eighth of an inch in diameter. The young scale-lice come out in the spring from underneath the female scales, and are minute and yellow. They crawl about for a while selecting new growth to fasten themselves to, or are carried to other trees on the feet of birds. On minute inspection, or with a glass, you may sometimes see mother and young traveling along like a hen and chickens.

On the older trees the scale is likely to remain on the twigs or small branches, but on young trees it may cover the entire tree, giving it the appearance of being coated with lime or ashes. It may attack the fruit, as well as the bark and leaves; and fruit so attacked shows a little purplish ring around each scale. Trees quickly die, whole orchards soon stand stark and dead, unless action be taken promptly. And not only do apple-trees suffer, but also other kinds of fruit trees as well as ornamental shrubs.

The infected apple-trees were fortunately not the only ones on the place, but they were young and well placed and we did not want to cut them down unless absolutely necessary. Some were dead, others were so advanced with the attack that cutting-down was really the only course, but still others we set out to save, and by dint of great cutting back and persistent spraying, while the trees were dormant, with a strong lime-sulphur-salt mixture, succeeded. Such a mixture may be bought, ready-mixed, of reputable dealers.

The success with the dreaded scale made us optimistic regarding the entire question of plant and tree enemies. It cannot be denied that it is a hard task, demanding constant labor and watchfulness, to battle successfully with the blighting fungus, the leprous scale, the insects that creep or crawl or walk or fly, that bite or chew or suck, but it can be done. And it is better to set out to do it than to watch things die and rail at fate in good set terms.

There is an offensive brute called a bagworm that destroys evergreens—it is said by scientists to be rare and wonderful. To our horror we found it on a number of trees, and at once set about making a collection of specimens—but not for science! We gathered a peck; and with that they have utterly disappeared.

To read long lists of plants and trees attacked, and bewilderingly longer lists of their foes, is needlessly depressing. That the loss to the country is three hundred million dollars annually and that, as a single example, there are two hundred kinds of insects that feed upon the grape alone, may all be true enough, but the situation is not so bad as all this would imply. In old English, "bug" meant "bugbear." "The bug which you would fright me with," says Hermione.

To fight the garden pests is a serious task, but far from a hopeless one. Assemble a few insecticides and fungicides, and draw upon this simple laboratory with knowledge and system, and you can kill the pests and shame the pessimist.

You should be ready to use Bordeaux mixture, a lime-and-sulphur scale-destroyer, a kerosene emulsion, tobacco dust, Paris green, and hellebore. With rare exceptions, these will be sufficient, and pests that they will not kill can be attacked by hand, by picking, pruning, or burning.

It should also be understood that there are natural enemies which destroy insects in myriad quantity; birds and snakes and toads and chickens and, perhaps even more, insect parasites; for, exemplifying the well-known rhyme, most pests have smaller pests to bite 'em, and so proceed ad infinitum. Pestilence, too, unexpectedly takes off enormous hosts of insects, just as the plague used to sweep off hosts of human beings.

And it was a wise man who remarked that good agriculture is itself the best of insecticides. Clean up after every crop; destroy all fallen fruit; keep dead wood and wood piles out of the orchard; strengthen your plants with fertilizer, for the stronger the plant the better it resists bugs and scale and fungus. Cultivate the ground thoroughly, for immense numbers of evil things, in the forms of larvæ and pupæ and eggs, are destroyed by opening them to air and sunlight. Rotate your crops, because some insects, not finding their favorite food, are not peckish enough to take up with something else but prefer to die.

But the fact must be faced that plants are attacked by an increased and increasing variety of foes. For this, civilization and commerce are responsible. An insect or a scale that used to stay quietly at home, in Asia or South America or Europe, is now carried to our shores as a stowaway passenger, and here, like other immigrants, thrives and multiplies. The San José scale thus entered California, and its course eastward has been traced, step by step, as historians trace the route of the Huns and Vandals. The gypsy moth and the codling moth came to us from Europe. The woolly aphis is a traveler from land to land. And pests which used to stay in one corner of our own country have been carried in shipments, especially of plants, to other parts. The potato-bug spread from Colorado, where it is still known as a practically innocuous insect. Many insects, especially in the form of caterpillars, have been traced as traveling along the roads by wagon, by automobile, by bicycle.

But it is not all insects, not all worms and bugs, that are bad. You may be entertaining angels unawares. The little ladybugs do no harm and a great deal of good, for they devour the plant lice. Ants are harmless, and excellent scavengers. I once heard a man actually complaining that his land was "infested with angle-worms"!—which do no harm and very greatly improve the soil. Every toad, old-fashioned farmers like to say, is worth ten dollars.

There is one thing to remember, for him who would grow great crops of fruit. Trees do not take care of themselves. What with trimming, pruning, spraying, mulching, digging around the roots, running wires in the holes after borers and worrying about field mice in winter, a fruit crop demands more care than does a garden or a field crop. And fruit is uncertain. One year or two years little or nothing, and perhaps in the third year a crop so great that one cannot begin to utilize it all, even though following determinedly the old axiom to eat what you can and what you can't you can. Not only are you unable to handle a big crop yourself—and it hurts you to see it actually waste—but you cannot even give it away, for after a while one learns that if you offer fruit, it is expected that you both gather it and deliver it! "Not without labor and perplexity to be given away," as some American writer expressed it, thus voicing the general tribulation.

And as to selling—well, like most people, we had no desire at all to attempt it; and in any case the world seems to have settled it, and it is rather an illogical condition, that although a man is at liberty to go from one to another, offering for sale, literally peddling, the most intimate products of his brain—an invention, a painting, a novel, a history, sermons, poems, plans for construction—he is not at liberty, unless his actual business is that of farming, to peddle the products of his land. He may peddle poems but not peaches, a picture but not asparagus. Unless, indeed, he is rich or titled, in which case he may sell anything on his place. It used to be said that King Edward sold live stock from Sandringham and whiskey from a distillery at Balmoral. The great nobles of Florence used to sell their farm produce, and even now, in corners of some of the palaces, are little shops with the sign "Cantina," where the wine and oil and charcoal of the present-day nobility are disposed of. In America, and especially in Eastern Pennsylvania, some of the very rich turn their thoughts to milk routes—and it is, to us, one of the mildly amusing features of life here, that when our cow runs dry our interim milkman is one of the wealthiest men of Philadelphia. We can always raise a gasp from a visitor by driving him past a huge mansion and remarking, casually, that it was built by our milkman!

With eleven acres, even though a great part of it is in trees and lawn, there ought to be the raising of forage crops: hay and clover and corn and rutabagas and millet for food, and rye-straw for bedding. Although it all seems a mystery at first, it is soon learned that one may grow millet in the early summer, plant rye and cut the next summer, while the timothy and clover are growing on the same field in the shelter of the rye straw.

We inherited a considerable quantity of wood from the trees chopped by our predecessor, for numerous logs were left that did not, like the stumps, defy saw and axe. With the fire-places, wood fires are kept freely blazing in winter, and the extensive alterations of the house made a wood-pile in themselves. Besides, from the many trees standing, there is a constant though minor supply of dropping branches,

such as made the quaint old versifier set down
so charmingly that "some brittle sticks of thorn
or briar make me a fire." And the residual
wood ashes are good for the land.

So steady a product may one have from the
chicken yard, that we have not had to buy a
single chicken or a single egg since coming here.
The cow, a Jersey, is fully self-supporting,
giving milk for the household and the chickens
and delicious cream and butter. It used to be
that, with old-action churns, it did not pay to
attempt butter-making for a small household,
from one cow. It was too tremendous a task.
But there are now little churns, of glass and
porcelain, with a dasher made to revolve so
simply that butter comes in a few minutes.
In the pasture grows an abundance of mushrooms.

Many a day practically every thing on the
table is from our own place. And these things
are such delicacies!—delicacies anyone may
have who will but live in the country: in May,
strawberries—no millionaire can have them
more delicious than with Jersey cream: in June,
red raspberries, with cream: in fall, peaches and
cream: and between fruit seasons, ice cream.

ADVENTURES IN HOME-MAKING

It really seems so worth while! And we can only repeat, that with the delicacies of really fresh fruits and vegetables and eggs and milk and broilers, there goes also the subtle quality that comes from its all having come as the result of your own plans and attention, and most likely in considerable degree from your own labor as well—a genial philosopher having well remarked that gardens raise not only fruits and vegetables but the average of human life.

There is a good deal of an idea that country living means only a coarse plenty—than which no mistake could be greater. There is plenty— that is assuredly a desideratum!—but it should be an epicurean plenty. Throughout, delicacy ought to be the ideal, and it is a charmingly attainable ideal: like brown broiler and green peas on a white plate. One ought not to desire the fat of the land so much as the cream of the land.

As winter comes on it is a pleasure to sum up the products from one's own place that await consumption. For the barn is full of hay, the corn-crib of corn, the chicken house of chickens; in the woodyard are great piles of wood; in covered trenches are celery, parsnips, cabbages, turnips and carrots; in the vegetable cellar are potatoes, sweet potatoes, winter squash and beets; in the store-room are mushrooms, dried on strings as in Italy, and there are jellies and jams and there are cans of strawberries, cherries, plums and pears and peaches. And anybody can go out and secure such results as readily as we have secured them.

CHAPTER XV

THE PICTURESQUE POSSIBILITIES OF THE BARNYARD

IT is really extraordinary, that the fierce men of the opening years of the French Revolution, busied as they were with war and blood and confiscation and extermination, should not only have had time and desire to turn to the rearrangement of the calendar, but should have performed the work with such delightful regard for Nature. It was just such a calendar as might have been adopted by a convention of avowed nature-lovers instead of a convention of some of the most daring and desperate men who have ever lived: and it seems to show that those men were intensely serious at heart, intensely bent on getting the entire scheme of the universe in accord with eternal verities.

There were Nivose, the month of snow, Pluviose, the month of rain, Ventose, the month of wind: there were the months of sprouts, of flowers, of pasture: there were Vendémiaire,

THE TRANSFORMING EFFECT OF STONE PILLARS AND PAINT

THE BARNYARD

Brumaire, Fromaire, vintage, fog, sleet—and it is odd to think that the famous 18th Brumaire, on which the supremacy of Napoleon was established, was simply the 18th day of the month of fog: there were the fruit month, the hot month, and Messidor, the harvest month.

An important point in regard to harvesting that did not occur to the earnest men who gave it a month, is that French barns have almost always an air of attractiveness; they are not the things of blighting unloveliness that they too often are in America—needless unloveliness, for there are picturesque possibilities in every barn-yard.

The general outline of the barn buildings of which we came into possession, however, was really excellent; two barns, near together, with twin gables; a carriage house adjoining; and between carriage house and the nearest barn a roofed-over space which is admirable to drive under for a shelter from storm—a highly important point forgotten by many a barn-builder.

This open shelter faced toward the side of the house, and the broad roof was upheld only by three tall and extremely insignificant iron posts, but these three slender posts were made into heavy and well-proportioned stone pillars by building rough stone around them, using the iron as a core. It took a man only two days and a half and cost only about ten dollars, and it is not too much to say that the result was transforming.

The cross-bracing up under the peaks of the twin gables—the queen-posts and tie-beams—were of the same dark color as the siding, but it was only the labor of a day to paint these peak-boards and all the trimming, white, and thus gain a fresh and cared-for appearance without painting the entire siding of the barns.

A rather bare spot was the side of the carriage house, and against this a broad ladder-trellis, for vines, was built, out of old material, including the curved pieces for the top, from an old and disused hop trellis that we found lying, where it had been blown down by the wind, in the tall grass near the pool.

A new window was put in the horse's stall, on the side facing in the same direction as the trellis, as the window already there was too small and faced toward the north—which the window of a horse's stall ought never to do. The new window is not only good for the horse but it also adds a touch of brightness to an otherwise shadowed corner.

A carpenter, coming to put in the window, and finding it low and broad, with two outswinging sash, said: "All right, but you need bars across, or the horse will break the glass."

Thereupon some old awning rods in the garret were thought of and brought down. "Just the thing," he said, "and easy to cut to length." Then he glanced from the bars to the window; "But they are not long enough!"

"Put them in vertical, then, not horizontal."

"Ah; of course!" And so the casement window was duly barred.

Between the two barns was an open space, seventeen feet wide, where the manure pile of previous occupancy had always been. This was promptly shut off by building a stone wall, six and a half feet high, across the front, making two isolated barns parts of the same group of buildings and not adding in the least to fire risk. It cost but very little, this stone wall, and adds to the good looks most markedly.

And, of course, trying to do proper farming so far as possible, no manure is accumulated there but is promptly spread on the land, and this stone-walled space is used for the stack of winter corn fodder and for a sunning spot where the cow may take the air in winter.

A huge walnut tree stands between house and barns and spreads its branches picturesquely over the broad shelter roof, and we set out a pair of nine-foot pyramidal privet bushes as a further leafy screen, beneath the lowest of the great walnut branches.

It is not too much to say that it is a glimpse of real picturesqueness, from the library door out towards the barn. And why not! It is all very well to philosophize abstractly about the useful being always beautiful from the mere fact of its serving a useful purpose; but that is a mere juggling of words. That the useful is often ugly, but that it ought to be as good-looking as one can possibly make it, is the truth of the matter.

Aiming at picturesqueness and at the same time at practical value, we wished our cow (we needed only one) to be a thoroughly good looker as well as a good milker, and therefore waited until the opportunity came to get a pedigreed Jersey, a handsome animal, giving a wonderful quality of milk. For a cow with grandmothers, like a horse with grandmothers, adds materially to the actual looks of a place, whether seen in the barn or in the pasture, and legitimately adds to one's sense of satisfaction. Once in possession, fine animals cost no more for maintenance and upkeep than do poorer ones.

Finding that our horse's hoofs were out of condition from having been driven too hard on city pavements, she was given a great deal of pasture life, was carefully shod, and, perhaps most important of all, the entire bottom of her box stall, great thick planking, was taken out, the edges and doorsill were concreted, and all the center was filled in with a deep layer of clay, over a foundation of broken stone: not ordinary clay, for this purpose, but brickmaker's clay, from a brickyard. The result has been that all trouble has disappeared and speed and looks have returned.

The cementing in the stall was done very easily, and much has been done in other places, here and there about the place. A friend, noticing this, likes to say: "I see you make cement flow like water!"—and it is indeed a wonderful and easily-handled medium. Cement enables one to think in stone; to carry out his thoughts and plans, in a permanent medium, almost as soon as thought and planned.

We cast the cement in a mold, by pouring it, wet, into a form made of boards, of precisely the desired shape and size and in precisely the location.

The favorite mixture in our work and the one with best results is one part of Portland cement, to two parts of sand, and four of stone, broken very small, or of cinders of the kind that one gets from power houses. The broken stone is first wetted: the cement and sand are well mixed, dry, and then stirred up with the wetted stone; then enough water is added to make the entire mixture a mushy mass—throughout, the mixing is done with a shovel, not a hoe— and then it is thrown into the mold, is well tamped, and is then allowed to stand till it is set, which will be next morning.

It is all so simple that unskilled labor can do it swiftly and well, except when the work is the making of such a thing as a doorstep, for that needs expert smoothing, with a coating of almost cement alone worked on. So often have we found cement helpful, that we could not think of such a thing as not having a bag of it constantly on hand and ready for use.

The hens, housed in the old cattle barn, are

given a yard of liberal range entirely hidden from house and drive, situated as the yard is beyond the barn and behind a group of fir trees. As a chicken yard cannot be made altogether good-looking, it is well to have it attractively hidden.

And even as it is the chicken yard is not really unpleasant, for there is a great deal of grass in it, the chickens having ample digging and dusting space besides, and there are a number of fruit trees, and it is bordered and overhung by evergreens. There is, too, a sun-catch arranged each winter—cornstalks awaiting their final fate in the cow's stall, leaning upon a rail supported on two low posts and thus keeping sweet and dry and shedding the rain and at the same time making an admirable sheltered place for the chickens on windy, chilly days.

A wood house, too, is in the chicken yard; and for this we had a long section of the old and demolished chicken house saved, in a single piece, with its rafters and shingles. It was drawn to the new yard, and built against the barn at the angle of a low pent-house roof, and under that all of our logs were piled, out of the rotting influences of rain and snow.

And when there came additional great quantities of wood, of all lengths and shapes and sizes, from the house alterations, the greater part was piled in the shape of a towering wigwam, which looks uniquely attractive while it lasts, and meanwhile feeds the fireplaces. One walks to it and takes off a stick just as, in England, one walks to the sideboard for a slice of cold roast.

A high fence was built with cedar posts and strong woven wire—not the thin-meshed kind usually sold—so that the boundaries of the yard should be fixed and permanent. For chickens must be securely fenced in so that they cannot injure the garden, and also to prevent their cultivating the habits of intimacy into which, uncurbed, they fall—haunting your front steps and lawn, roosting on the foot-scraper and tumbling over your feet as you walk.

At the most prominent corner of the barn, nearest the house, grows a great crimson rambler. Along the chicken-yard fence, and against the gray stone wall and the side of the barns, we set out rows of martial hollyhocks. Constantly our aim has been to have charm of appearance without detracting from usefulness.

LOOKING FROM THE DUTCH DOOR TO THE ALTERED BARN

THE BARNYARD

But one kind of picturesqueness did not appeal and that was the picturesqueness of stanchions. For a stanchioned cow suffers greatly. The time will certainly come when societies for the prevention of cruelty will see to it that prohibitive laws are passed against such pilloried pain. Meanwhile, those who use stanchions ought to go the logical step further and, like the Dutch, tie the cow's tail to the ceiling so that she shall not waste her milk-producing strength in swishing flies.

We have a few pigeons and they are a pleasant feature, with their bowing and preening, and their soft cooing in the early morning, and their splashing in the basin of the fountain.

The intention, at the first, was to have not only a few pigeons, but a great many, and so half of one of the barn lofts was screened off with meshed wire, and a pigeon-fly was made outside. Following due precautions and rules, the increase in pigeons should be almost as great as that of Josh Billings' cats, which could be counted upon to yield each year something like eight hundred per cent.

But the pigeons gradually disappeared, and the anticipated increase became unanticipated decrease. Some flew away, others squabbled instead of squabbing and had to be eaten, and only a few would lay, although, after consulting a pigeon specialist, they were fed with such delicacies as lettuce in January. Most of such squab as actually appeared were eaten by rats. And we realized, rather late, that the mesh-wire in the loft, which had been put up with the sole thought of keeping the pigeons in, was not of small enough mesh to keep rats out. The pigeons are homers and the few that we now have were born here and survived, and they therefore need no wire to teach them domesticity.

There were some rats about the barn when we came but we paid no particular attention to them. And then, all unintentionally, we added to their number!

For we had put two acres in rye, and had had it piled in the loft without threshing, as it would have been too impracticable and expensive to do otherwise with so small a crop, and our plan was to throw it down to the dry ground, in bunches, for the chickens to eat the grain out of it, and then to have it used as bedding for the stable. But the rats so attacked that rye that in a short time they had stripped off every particle of grain, and the food supply caused such increase of number that in a short time they had completely overrun the barns. When other ways were closed to them, they went up the water spouts and dug holes through the shingle roof. They defied such simple things as glass broken in their runnels. Traps, after a few catches, they laughed at; a house terrier was helpless against myriad creatures who climbed and tunneled; poison about a chicken yard and barn would be too dangerous. Yet something had to be done.

Then a chemist came to the rescue. He told of a particular chemical, and of how to mix it with some mushy food, such as a breakfast food. "Put it where nothing but rats can get at it. They will eat it eagerly, but in its mushy state will not carry any away. Don't let it stand after it stiffens. If it gets into the hay it would kill the horse. And of course it would kill the chickens if fragments should be carried where they will ever go."

Well, seventy-three corpses were counted and buried, and we knew there were many who ran away to die, and the barn was cleared, and with no further loss than that of one single guinea hen. And should we ever have a field of rye again, it will be cut green before the forming of the grain upon the straw.

It seemed to us that a couple of China geese, with their dignified walk, a veritable "goose-step," and their peculiarly striking heads, add picturesqueness to a place, and so our couple are allowed to wander from pool to barnyard at will. In the matter of eggs, however, geese are a decided disappointment. They lay only a few, along in late winter and early spring, and for the rest of the year merely strut and swim and wear their whitest of feathers.

A few guineas, too, add a touch of interest; and they are not only dependable layers, but are much more likable fowl than ordinary chickens. They always lay their eggs in curiously hidden nests somewhere outside—they are essentially wild fowl, and do not do well if their wings are clipped to keep them in bounds—but their nests are sure to be happened upon, and usually have a great many eggs in them. A point that gains them a place above chickens is that when one of their number is hurt, the others stay by it and try to help it, or at least offer it the comfort of companionship, whereas when a chicken is hurt all its companions turn upon it and rend it cruelly, or at the least at once desert it.

There is so much that is charming that is naturally connected with a barn and a barn-yard, that it is really wrong not to follow up the advantages and make everything as attractive as possible. The sweet-smelling hay-lofts, the barred corn-crib displaying its yellow treasure, the wavering little calf in the springtime, the coops where little chickens flutter in and out and where, precisely as in the beginning of the world, the hen gathers her chicks under her wing—all is attractiveness.

CHAPTER XVI

THE ALTERATION OF THE SIDE OF THE HOUSE

FROM the moment of acquisition, it was determined to make material alteration of the exterior of the house. It was not enough to plan adjustment and rearrangement of the interior. The general ineffectiveness, or worse, of the outside was a tantalization; it demanded change.

It was the western side that first had attention, as considerable part of the needed alterations, there, had to be done in connection with the alteration of the interior.

The house, on account of its relation to the public roads, may be approached either up the hill from the front, or down the slope from behind, and this puts every part of its exterior, front and back and sides, into possible view. This arrangement of the roads, giving access from both directions, is of very great convenience, for we find that people use one approach just about as much as the other.

THE SIDE OF THE HOUSE, AS WE FOUND IT

THE SIDE OF THE HOUSE

And so, here was one of the roads curving toward a rear corner of the house, and thence continuing, by our own drive, right under the western wing. And this approach, even from the time of the initial sight of it, filled us with despair.

There was the protrusive disfigurement of a monstrously ugly bay window; there was the blemish of a jutting, jig-saw, covered stoop, with mincing steps leading down to the ground— the under part of this stoop being a dog-kennel· there was an outside entrance to the cellar, topped with ugly flaps; there was a hungriness, a thinness of aspect, about the roof line and garret—but this last could not be satisfactorily remedied except by the broad gables that were to come later as part of the alterations of the front. There was the general meagerness, unsatisfactoriness, commonness, that came from that side of the house being very high set with nothing to relieve the bare tallness of the foundations.

But fine trees lined the outside of the drive, ready to give their charm to whatever improvements should be attempted. In spite of present unprepossessingness, there were pleasurable possibilities.

ADVENTURES IN HOME-MAKING

The first thing to do was to close up the cellar-way.   It was not the only outside cellar entrance, so it was not at all needed.   A wall of stone, flush with the main wall of the cellar, was quickly built by a mason, the rough stone foundations of the cellar steps giving him the material. And such things are so easily done!—although so many people dread them, as threateningly arduous and expensive, and let disfigurements remain for years or, it may be, forever.

The outside of the walled stair space was now filled in, with a large amount of rubbish at the bottom and a depth of good garden soil at the top.

In place of the unsightly bay, there were to be two banks of windows, with three windows in each bank, one set of windows for the first floor and the other for the second.   The covered stoop was to be cleared away, and, in place of the door opening from it into the kitchen, there was to be a window.

We bought the banks of windows direct from a mill, sending a home-made drawing of what we wanted, with dimensions.   They cost, delivered at our railway station, fifty-two dollars. This even included glass, as the shipment was from Ohio, and the Ohio custom is to send glass with sash, whereas Pennsylvania mills send sash unglazed.

Then the contractor who had done much of the interior alterations of the house offered to put in these big three-part windows, and also to take off the stoop and put in a new kitchen window, and to change the laundry door, for only seventy-five dollars. Thus, for a total of one hundred and twenty-seven dollars, the side of the house was totally changed in looks, although in advance the work had seemed very much more formidable.

Yet it was not done quite so easily and smoothly as it might seem from merely reading it.

The mill sent the windows "K.D."—knocked down; taken apart and put in small compass for shipping—and the carpenter did not discover, until the side of the house was torn out, that two windows of the six were of wrong size, and that the house must be roughly boarded in till the right size could be made and shipped from that distant mill.

Then when the right size came, "This will all be closed in in just one day!" said the contractor cheerily, "so there will be no trouble about

[317]

shutting up the house to-night." But some-how—it was impossible to know just why—it was pretty much open to breezes and burglars for five days!

The laundry, at the end, was not quite so wide as the rest of the wing, although there had been no reason whatever for this annoying differ-ence; and now, to make it uniform, its roof was built out to the edge, giving a most con-venient sheltered place there at the laundry door, which had now become the rear entrance of the house. To form a wall for this sheltered space, and to continue the line of the side of the house, a square-mesh trellis of wood was built.

Painting, on this side of the house, was not at present to be done, except where imperatively needed for temporary protection of the wood, for the forthcoming alteration of the front of the house was to include this as part of one general scheme.

Inside the roofed-over space at the back door are kept fire-hose and reel, ready to connect with the fire-plug, which is fortunately at the bend of the road, one hundred feet away, with high pressure—for this is outside of the city

limits, and, although there is always a picturesqueness in seeing volunteer fire companies
go tearing over the roads from more or less
distant points and converging toward a fire,
and although they do work enthusiastically,
there is always and necessarily some delay
involved, and it is a good thing for the country
dweller to be ready to do what he can before
they arrive.

By the taking away of bay window, stoop and
cellarway, and setting out the line of the laundry,
a straight, good line was secured for the entire
side of the house, which was just what we had
aimed at. For a width of ten feet along the
side, garden soil was put in, and twenty of the
best and largest of the flowering shrubs from
the front lawn were planted, as the work of
the side of the house was intentionally done in
time and season to have the place ready for
them. The shrubs next to the wall were
trimmed down to window-sill height, and afterward kept trimmed there, except beside the
trellis, where they were permitted to grow taller.
In front of this line of shrubs we set a line of
lower ones, and in front of them chrysanthemums; and thus, in all, not only completely

relieved the former bareness, with this banked mass of greenery from the drive's edge right up to the windows, but gave also a sequence of color throughout the season: with the pale yellow of early Forsythia, the red of Pyrus Japonica and the accompanying white of deutzia and bridal-wreath, the white of hardy hydrangeas, deepening slowly into bronze, and finally the glorious medley of color of the chrysanthemums. And in the broad space occupied by these shrubs and flowers there had not, before, been even the slightest touch of greenery; not even a single blade of grass.

Nor was this all that the transplanted shrubs did for us; for many were set out in a grouping fifty feet long, in a sunny and suitable spot near the turning of the public road, and besides them, as a marginal hedging, were planted a mass of formal dahlias and the fascinatingly informal four-o'clocks.

Leading from the back doorstep of the house is a line of stepping-stones; a picturesque kind of path, easily made, that has been laid at several stretches around house and barn; flat stones, not too large and not in any way shaped up, laid with a space of a few inches between each and on a level with the surface of the ground, so that when grass grows up between and around the stones the lawn mower may be run smoothly over them. Other stones are inset, on edge, to divide the shrub-and-flower bed from the drive.

Through the laundry roof projected a piece of stove-pipe for chimney, and it so uncannily suggested immediate need for the fire-hose that it was taken down and a real chimney built instead. And it was made of a kind to match properly an old-time house; for it is of rough stone, built up on the outside of the laundry, from the ground itself to a height of fifteen feet. It looks at least a hundred years old, as the stone that was used was well weathered; and the mason, taking pride in his work, added a clever touch of his own. He had a mysterious paper bag with him, from which, when the chimney was built and before the mortar had set, he blew and scattered a black powder by which the mortar marvelously was blackened and aged. It was scrapings from the forge chimney of a blacksmith shop! The first rain carried off all the unattached and superfluous dust, and the entire effect became that of a piece of stonework weathered and darkened by the slow hands of Time.

The total cost for the labor, the stone being furnished from the place, was only eight dollars; and from time to time these prices are mentioned to point out, practically, how easily the apparently difficult or impossible may be accomplished.

Yet the result did not in the least please the mason's assistant, for, his ideal being the new and sharp-sided and trig, he shook his head deploringly and remarked to his chief that it looked as if the stones had merely been thrown at the chimney!

The approaching public road, here, is bordered delightfully by low stone walls and lines of avenued trees. We did not want to put a gate across the roadway to mark off our own; it would have been both inhospitable and inconvenient; but we had two substantial posts of stone built, one on each side, to indicate the entrance. We did not want them to look large and feudal, as if containing a watchman and arquebus—we have seen that kind!—but only solid and sufficiently substantial, and so had them made four-square, measuring two feet six inches on each side, with a flat cap, of stone, three inches projective. And as for the height, the mason was stopped at the precise point— five feet, six inches—that seemed proportionately right for looks.

On the side of each post dangles a heavy chain, of graduated links, the two chains being precisely alike, even to a knotting, and a twisting change of link, at the lower ends. And both these hand-wrought chains were found on the place!—being attached to a great heavy wagon-pole from some wagon that was worn out years ago, and the pole having been thrown away beside the brook. Yet they look, black-painted, as if they had been definitely made and matched for their new purpose of hanging on stone entrance posts! Over and over again one is made to realize two things: one, the importance of disposing of, getting out of sight, clearing away, everything that is really useless—and this clearing away is something that we ourselves do unhesitatingly and constantly—and the other is the holding fast to whatsoever is adaptable, and seeing to what use it can best be put; a use that is likely to be something very different from what its maker intended.

Up the heart of each post is a length of pipe, for the putting in of electric wires for a light on the top of each post, some time in the future. The pipe was on hand, and the building of it in cost nothing extra; whereas, were one to wish pipes put in after such posts were built it would be utterly impossible, and the only expedient would be to use some surface contrivance with outside wires.

The draft of the cooking range had always been so extremely good—a vital point of happiness to a home-maker—that we could not but ascribe its excellence to a tall galvanized iron stack on top of the chimney. We had always deplored the presence of that stack, for it managed to be so constantly in evidence, even from a distance, through the trees. But it seemed a case of not quarreling with necessity —the necessity presumably arising from the presence behind the house of the wind-break.

But one day, in a high wind, a guy-wire snapped and the chimney top tilted rakishly, threatening to fall with results disastrous, and giving promise of work for mason and iron man; and our colored youth, going up to investigate, worked his way along the high ridge, stood

THE SIDE OF THE HOUSE, AS IT NOW APPEARS

beside the chimney at the extreme end, reached toward the broken strand, slipped slightly— and, instinctively clasping his arm around the base of the stack, found it crumbling in his grasp! "I jest squez!" he gasped. However, he balanced himself and did not fall; the stack was a thing of the past; and the kitchen range, with stackless chimney, draws as well as ever it did.

There were fantastic crenelations along all the ridges, including even those of the dormers; crenelations of galvanized iron, ill-favored, disfiguring, in fact positively ugly, and peculiarly undesirable from their place of prominence. It was feared that to take them off would injure the roof and cause leakage, but at least an experimental effort had to be made. And they came off by mere breaking! It was only necessary to take one in the hand, and bend it slowly back and forth a few times, to make it snap off:—and thus with two hours of work the ridges were cleared and the house immensely benefited, and ridge and roof were not a particle hurt.

In the amount of change necessary, the eastern side of the house was very different from the western, for it needed little to be done except what was to come in connection with the alteration of the house-front. There was no bareness of foundation to counteract, the land being higher here. The little portico at the library door needed new wooden posts, and it was also given a flooring of brick and a new step—this step, seven feet long, being of concrete. That was one thing that had become a rule: to have every outside step either of cement or brick or stone, for the sake of strength and permanency of appearance; for few things give such an air of cheapness, paltriness, inferiority, as weak-looking steps.

From the center of the roof of this little portico hangs an old-fashioned watchman's lantern, of really perfect shape and proportion, showing, as so many things show, the unconscious artistic accuracy so often displayed by even the humble artisans of the past. This is but a simple punched lantern, of sheet iron, with its rounded body full of holes. It is made for a candle. Perhaps some town watch of olden time carried it on his nightly rounds, or perhaps it was used by some farmer to go to his barn or lead his family through the darkness of a winter's night to church. We have two such lanterns—

they can be fitted easily with an electric light or with gas—and the other one is kept for use indoors, being even better than this, square in shape and cross-barred. Were some Benvenuto Cellini to wish a homely lantern he could not well make one of better proportion, design or shape than either of these two.

From the portico a path leads toward the barn, a path thick-bordered with flowers. In earliest spring it is a daffodil path; later it is a peony path, for here were the gorgeous peonies carried from their ill-placed bed in the front lawn; and there are also columbines and dwarf marigolds, white phlox and blue delphiniums and the radiant glory of oriental poppies. "But those poppies last for only a few days," once remarked a visitor critically. As if the briefness of a delicate pleasure could be cause for belittlement!

One is always seeing how much can be done with flowers, and what fine and varying results may be secured. For instance, the east lane, the entrance by which one approaches directly to the front of the house, is not only bordered by gray stone walls and lines of avenued trees, as is the other road mentioned, but it is also, throughout its length of two hundred feet, lined on either side with white altheas, set there by some flower-lover of the past.

And, although there is perhaps no tangible reason for it, it is always reminiscent of the long-ago Colonel Lovelace, this combination of stone walls and charming Althea.

CHAPTER XVII

MAKING A TERRACED FRONT WITH WHITE COLUMNS

AND now we had come to the last work of all; and not only the last but the most important, the most significant, and by far the largest and the most costly. And yet the comparative ease with which it was done and the comparatively small sum that it required, compared with the value of the result attained, shows that no one need fear to attempt to alter radically his house if alteration means improvement. If it could be done successfully with this house, in Colonial style, it could be done successfully with almost any house, in the style best suited to its architecture and to its owner's taste. If there would be æsthetic and financial betterment, do not hesitate. *Audace, audace, toujours audace!*

Our task was nothing less than to transform absolutely the entire front. In place of a mixture of stone center and frame wings, dormer roof and ugly gables, there were to be uniformity, homogeneity, beauty. At least, that was what we planned; that was what we visualized. The entire house was apparently to be stone, and there was to be a brick-terraced, green-shuttered, white-pillared front.

In the previous alterations there had been schemes requiring the spending of now ten dollars, now fifty dollars, now a hundred and fifty. In all, scattered as they were over a considerable time, the sums might almost be looked upon as current expenses. But now, all at once we were under different conditions. Here was confrontation with an expense of a large number of hundreds, all at one time. But it was to be faced precisely as if it were making an addition to the purchase price—which, indeed, it essentially was.

From the first it was a house of possibilities. That, after all, is what is vital. For houses are like men: it is not what they are that counts, but what they may become.

The house, two stories and a garret in height, was sixty-six feet long; yet it was not nearly so large as this would imply, as, to take advantage of the sweeping view, it was a house of frontage without depth. And this unusual proportion of frontage gave it, so long as the front was bad, an unusual proportion of undignified ugliness; the compensatory condition being that if we should succeed in making it dignified and attractive it would have, for its size, an unusual proportion of dignity and attractiveness. It was certainly worth trying for.

The central portion was of stone, plastered; the most familiar and characteristic type of old-time house in this region. At each end was a wooden, clapboard wing, shapelessly gabled, and meager as to its eaves. In front of the entire house stretched an insignificant porch, one story high, without even the dignity of width. The problem was to make the entire front one consistent Colonial whole; Colonial, because that was our personal preference in American architecture, and because every point thus far, in our alterations and furnishing, had been along strictly Colonial lines. A house ought not to be a meaningless medley.

The center section was thoroughly good, although it was hard to realize this, hemmed in as it was with unproportioned unattractiveness. That it was of plastered stone rather than unplastered was not a defect, even if it had not been in accord with local standards, for to have the entire house plastered, alike the wooden wings and the stone center, was essential if we were to gain homogeneousness. And there was far more than plastering to do!

Here was the proposition. The alteration of the front, if successful, would add beauty and dignity; it would add immensely to our personal satisfaction and enjoyment. But we were not in a position to enter into heavy expense for the sake of æsthetic or intellectual satisfaction alone.

Then here was the further consideration. Should the work be successful, should the result accord with our visualization, some thousands of dollars would be added in actual value. True, it would not be practical and realized value unless we should sell or rent; until then it would be locked-up value. But it would be locked up in our own possession, daily contributing to our happiness. And in what way could the amount of money be laid out to better practical advantage than in adding to the value of our property? Of course, had the house been in a neighborhood of retrograding values, expensive alterations might have been unwise. But, as it was, the neighborhood was advancing even more than we could have anticipated.

Even after deciding that the entire front must be altered, it was a long and dubitative question to fix upon what would be precisely the best looking and most practicable change. For there were a number of ways possible, and each would give a Colonial result. There were varied potentialities with roof and porch and pillars. We might have one single portico in the middle or one at each end; we might have pillars one-story high or two; we might even do without any pillars at all. Our aim was to combine maximum of effect with comparative minimum of expense.

We took time to it, thinking, studying and discussing, for it was to be the completing work of all and decision did not have to be hastily made. Thus it was that the picture of pure white and deep green, of tall pillars, of porticoed ends, of dignity of terrace, was gradually evolved. But, once evolved, once really recognized as the best, for this house and this location, there was no longer hesitation.

Thus far, in the many different alterations,

inside and outside, that we had taken up, we had not called in the aid of an architect. It had been work that we could do better without an architect's help, for it was made up of a multitude of things, dependent upon our own desires and fancy, that could not have been satisfactorily handled by any but ourselves. Here, with this final and most important work, the result had still to be precisely what we planned and visualized, but we could be materially aided by an architect's practical knowledge of details in making plans and specifications to submit to contractors; there was needful a considerable amount of technical description, and of definite measures and heights, for without it bids could not be made, nor a contract entered into, without the certainty of misunderstanding. We knew, for example, that we wished certain pillars, two stories high, but we did not know how to specify those pillars technically, to be sure of getting what we wanted from a carpenter or mill.

In all our planning, we tried to avoid the mistaken viewpoint of those who, with incomparable complacency, say, "I know what I like!" without for a moment realizing that

THE NEW FRONT OF THE HOUSE, IN PROGRESS

the important thing is first to make sure that it ought to be liked. For at least we did not decide without long and careful effort to come at the best.

Hawthorne somewhere expresses the idea, through one of his characters, that the ideal way is so to build the exterior of a house that it shall remain forever the same, leaving each generation to alter the interior, in turn, to suit its own taste and convenience: the exterior going on adding venerableness to its original beauty. We aimed to do this with our own house so far as it could be done; for to the extent that the exterior possessed beauty we were to leave it untouched to gain new venerableness, and we planned to alter only those parts which were added excrescences.

The eave line of the center of the house was of precisely the right height; its roof was at precisely the right angle; its dormers were perfectly placed. So we determined that the roof line and cornice line of the center should be continued right on to each end of the house and that at each end there should be a portico, two stories high, with four white pillars as supports for each.

The entire plan was laid before an architect. He looked it over, and then came out and looked at the house. He declared the plan to be quite feasible, and carefully estimated that it would cost, in all, not over fifteen hundred dollars.

This was so delightfully reasonable as to permit of our going ahead, and we were ready to face a slightly greater total than this, knowing that a preliminary estimate must always fall somewhat short.

It seemed best, for this work, not to follow the rule that in our numerous minor alterations had proved so excellent; that of taking up one part at a time; for here all the different kinds of work were to be so closely bound up with one another, so mutually involved, as to make one single work of it all. It would be impracticable to contract with carpenter, painter, bricklayer, stonemason, plasterer, lather, separately, the work being indivisible.

Bids were asked for: and then came our surprise! For the lowest involved a total expenditure, including the architect's commission, of about one thousand dollars more than the estimate. However, our hearts were now set on it, and as it was distinctly worth while as a financial proposition, even with this added cost, we decided to go ahead.

The bids had been asked for in a "not to exceed" form, because work that is not new work and that is not clear-cut and straightaway, is naturally enough looked upon with somewhat of dubiousness by contractors, as they fear unexpected complications from adjusting and connecting new work with old. However, the cost ran to the limit after all, and "not to exceed" became "not to be less than." At the same time, however, the contract was so phrased as to provide absolutely against possible extras.

Somehow, when one is busied with important home-making work, it is pleasant to think that Shakespeare thought of it all, and expressed it in as modern a way as if he were a playwright of the twentieth century, spending the royalties of to-day. For he wrote:

> "When we mean to build,
> We first survey the plot, then draw the model,
> And, when we see the figure of the house,
> Then must we rate the cost of the erection;
> Which if we find outweighs ability,
> What do we then, but draw anew the model
> In fewer offices, or, at last, desist
> To build at all?"

But we did not want to "desist to build at all"; we wanted to "see the figure of the house" in realization.

That the wings were of different widths, one being just two feet wider than the other, that neither of them was of the same width as the center, and that one, that of the library, was too narrow for our ideal of a portico, marked the first difficulty, for it made it impossible to do what would otherwise have been the natural way: that is, have each portico the precise width of the wing behind it.

The first detailed drawing that was submitted showed porticoes narrow and peaked and slim, with pillars too slender for height. It was cause for despair. And it was not sufficient for mollification to represent that the portico in front of the library must from necessity be narrow and must thus control the width of both.

For the home-maker who would get what he requires, learns not to accept adverse dicta too hastily; he learns that "must" is an excellent word for what he wants but decidedly the reverse of excellent for what he does not want. It bears within itself a challenge.

The problem was mulled over again. To

begin with, it was evident that these white-pillared porticoes must be of equal width, and also that each must have its peak over the middle of the group of windows beneath it; thus making each portico concentric, as an architect would call it. The façade of this particular house, before the changes in it, seemed to favor the eccentric rather more than the concentric, however.

But the clarifying idea at last came. It seemed complete and satisfactory, and we put it before the architect. It was, that the space for the portico on the narrow wing should be widened two feet, by extending the front wall of the house, by means of a false wall, one foot farther along, thus permitting of a balancing and additional foot on the other side of the necessary center of this portico. Then the other portico could likewise be increased two feet, for there was leeway there. And so, with both porticoes, four feet in all would thus be gained.

This additional four feet was just what was needed. And when drawings were again made, still showing over-slender columns and still a general effect of peaked narrowness, it was pointed out to the architect that this was now entirely unnecessary, for by giving greater diameter to the pillars and decreasing the peaked height of the pediment by keeping it sufficiently below the main ridge of the roof, it should now be quite possible to have all the proportions pleasing. In fact, this had to be insisted upon; peakedness and narrowness would be fatal. After all, pillared structures had been a special fancy of ours, and we had been observing them for years—Greek temples, French public buildings, old American houses—and we felt that it was not unreasonable to insist upon having what we wanted, now that at length we were to have a pillared house of our own.

Throughout, we aimed at simplicity. This made the choice fall upon plain pillars rather than fluted ones, principally because the plain shafts would give enough up and-down lines, with the eight pillars, without adding to this lined effect with the vertical groovings of fluted columns. Nor would we have pilasters on the wall, for we feared that they would give the effect of a forest of masts, like two four-posters in a bedroom. We feared the fussy.

The pillars are of white pine, and of what

is known as lock-joint type, thus making them as nearly crack-proof as wooden pillars can be made. They are hollow: this being the modern type, and much cheaper than the antique solid ones.

A highly important point in their arrangement is that they are not equally spaced, in two sets of four, but instead are in four sets of two, and are thus very much more effective.

Each pillar measures fifteen and a half feet in height, including the capital and plinth— the plinth of each being a smoothly finished stone four inches thick. Above the tops of the columns is eight feet of superimposed entablature, two feet of which is frieze, very plain, the sole ornaments being a triglyph over each column —"triglyph" being one of those esoteric words with a very simple meaning; a triglyph being merely a board with three scratches on it!— not more than three, or it would be remindful of a lady whom we heard, at St. Mark's, regretting that the Quadriga had now only four horses, the wicked Napoleon having taken the fifth and sixth to Paris. The width of each portico is twenty feet, thus closely approaching the total height. The pillars are Doric in design.

The continuation of the general roof line necessarily produced a broadly generous gable on each side of the house, one over the side windows of the dining-room and the other over the side of the library. The library side, too, was affected by the extra foot of new and hollow wall, which deeply and delightfully recessed the library windows and door.

The front door, in itself, was all that we could desire, being heavy, low, six-panelled, broad. But its original pent-house had been taken off when the long wooden porch was built, and now the removal of the porch would leave it without protection, opening directly upon the terrace. So a slightly projecting entablature, with plain pediment covered with a narrow shingle roof, was built, with two simple pilasters outlining the door; all this fitting the door to its new environment.

Along the entire front of the house is a brick-paved terrace, thirteen feet wide, its level being six inches lower than the sill of the front door. The foundations are deep, and the walls are of stone and eighteen inches thick.

Fortunately there was plenty of stone on the place, from a number of disused walls that it had been necessary to tear down. Stone walls that border roads, and stone walls dividing fields of radically different character, are to us so altogether desirable that it is hard even to imagine a vandalism that would needlessly destroy them. There are long lengths of such wall here, and they are proudly preserved as precious. But there were also crisscross walls that were certainly worse than useless through dividing where there was now nothing to divide and looking ill from being absolutely and awkwardly in the way. Such walls it was necessary to tear down, and they furnished material for various work about the place, and most of all for the stone needed for this long terrace.

These aimless walls were built, so tradition has it, by an owner of some three-quarters of a century ago, who, accustomed to look too steadily (or unsteadily) at the local substitute for wine when it was red, used always to berate himself for the over-indulgence, and, while recovering from it, always set out to do penance by building another section of wall.

A work that could not be done until all of the structural work was completed was the plastering; and this plastering was to be the main agent in metamorphosing the house into final harmony, final homogeneousness. Carpenter and mason had carried out plans for transposing the shape of the building, and now the plasterer was to transform, apparently, the very substance.

The house, alike the center and the wings, was to be coated with plaster over all its surfaces, on front and back and sides. Everywhere it was to look like a structure of plastered stone. It was no longer to be a hodgepodge, partly frame and partly stone.

The old plaster, on the central portion, was hacked to secure a key for the new; the clapboarding on the front of the wings was torn off, so that the plaster coat should be of uniform surface with that of the center; the sides and rear of the wings were furred and lathed; and the plaster was rounded in at each window-frame with great care.

The plaster was of fresh-burned lime, good sand, and clean cattle-hair; the sand for the first coat being clean bar-sand, and for the second coat, which was not put on till the first was completely dry, white sand. The second coat was so heedfully mixed and applied as not only to give a thoroughly fine white color to the house, instead of a white with the grayish tinge so often seen on plastered houses, but also to avoid dullness and dampness of aspect on a rainy day. For the plastering contractor was like the other contractors—the carpenter, the painter, the mason—and felt a personal pride and personal interest in the result of the work, and we feel that this general co-operation had much to do with the final result.

The painting of the woodwork was the final work of all. There were three coats of it, and it gave the needed glow of color and the sense of a finished task. It is a simple color scheme; it is only a green and a white—a pure white, not a pearly or creamy or gray; and the green is a green that is not either yellow or blue. The picturesque solid shutters are green and the doors are green; the door frames and the window-sash are white, the cornice and the columns are white, the mass of the house, plastered, is white. And as we mount the hill toward the house, and see it gleaming among the trees, we feel quite Horatius-like, in looking at the white porch of our home.

CHAPTER XVIII

THE REALIZATION

AND so it was finished. And it had been so delightfully worth while! We had dreamed a dream and the dream had come true.

The house, glimmering white among the green trees of the hillside, stands for two years of constant striving toward an end; not two years of house alteration exclusively, but also of coincident and varied occupations. In the house alteration we had tried to follow where our fancies led. We had fixed upon an ideal and had set out to secure it, and had gone economically along the road we could afford to travel.

We had learned many things in the course of these busily occupied years. We learned how infinitely precious is a home that has been planned for, labored for, wrought in every part into intimate and personal relationship. We learned that luck may be counted among one's resources. We learned that it is possible to se-

THE REALIZATION

cure romance, tempered by practicality. We learned that ordinary means are sufficient to secure results. We learned that wealth, however delightful, is not indispensable. And, indeed, if one will but look he may see this truth expressed in a thousand different forms. We have a glass bottle, picked up for two cents on a stall in a back street of Naples—a thing of beauty and grace. We have two lovely pieces of Sèvres, absolutely unmarred, certified personally to us, by the curator of the Sèvres Museum, as having been made imperially for the Tuileries and as having been lost from there when the palace was sacked and destroyed—and the two pieces cost but ten francs at the Marché du Temple. And to go from pennies and francs to dollars, this entire place, adding cost of alterations to original purchase price, represents only such an investment as could be handled by the average American.

Thoreau loved to remark that whenever he passed one of those big tool-boxes beside the railroad track, the thought came to him that therein were all the requisites of a home. But Thoreau was setting forth only one of those half-truths in which he took perverse delight.

ADVENTURES IN HOME-MAKING

For beauty is worth while and comfort is worth while and to be surrounded by the precious things one loves is worth while. The tool-box theory of life has too many shortcomings.

Happy the man whose wish and care a few suburban acres bound! To live near enough to the city to be of the city, and yet far enough in the country to be of the country—somehow, that seems to be worth trying for. And there is still room for all who care for it. The time may come when the increase of population will cause country suburbs to vanish or to be so far away as to lose some desirable characteristics, but at least that time is far distant. We remember a letter, or a record in some old-time memoirs, expressing the firm conviction of some nobleman of the eighteenth century that all Paris would be practically depopulated by the rush of people to country homes; and Napoleon himself used to declare that there would be only a continuous city along the Seine from Paris to Havre. But it is more than a century since Napoleon said this, and a pleasant boat ride will still, within less than a single hour, take one from Paris and set him among trees and flowers and sylvan charm. And in the vicinity of every American city—yes, even New York!—there are still many and many opportunities for the home-maker.

A home should represent the maker of it. No place like home!—an admirable sentiment, this, if interpreted in terms of individuality. For a man ought to make his home so different from the home of everyone else that he may rightly say there is none other like it. There are no two personalities alike; therefore there should be no two homes precisely alike.

To own a house is a laudable ambition. But to make your house distinctively your own is an ambition more laudable still. In other words, getting a building and a certain amount of land round about it is one thing, and it is quite another to make that land and that building individually representative.

"To be happy at home," writes Doctor Johnson, with that phraseological formality which was never sufficient to conceal the wisdom of his thought; "to be happy at home is the ultimate result of all ambition; the end to which every enterprise and labor tend, and of which every desire prompts the prosecution;" and to be happy at home ought to be possible if the kind of home one dreams of has been made, and if Fate permits it to be retained.

Whatever we have done may be done by any who fix upon their ideal and, with perseverance and enthusiasm and a fair degree of good fortune, labor for it. Difficulties usually vanish or become petty when approached with confidence. Bunyan quaintly writes that the way to the House Beautiful was barred by two lions, that frightened and turned back the pilgrims, Mistrust and Timorous—but that the lions were really chained, and that the path to the House Beautiful was therefore open to all who did not causelessly fear.

When we first looked over our house, two years ago, wondering whether we should make it our home, it was clear that it would demand both faith and works: a very strong faith and a great deal of work. But also, from the first, it was evident—and that was the saving grace of it all—that there were possibilities. "Hope told a flattering tale." We took the house. We planned, we contrived, we visualized. And the substance of things hoped for became gradually clear, and the evidence of things not seen was justified.

MABEL TUKE PRIESTMAN

Art and Economy in Home Decoration
Profusely Illustrated. Cloth. $1.50 net. Postage 15 cents.

The Studio Year Books of Decorative Art
These Year Books are issued as supplements to *The International Studio*, which the N. Y. *Tribune* says *"is by all odds the most beautiful art magazine printed in English,"* and are valuable guides to the artistic construction, decoration and furnishing of the home. Each volume contains hundreds of illustrations, many in color, of the work of the leading architects, designers, and craftsmen of Great Britain and the Continent.

Year Book of 1906:—*Cloth 4to. $5.00 net. Postage 35 cents.*
Year Book of 1907:—*Cloth 4to. $10.00 net. Postage 35 cents.*
Year Book of 1908:—*Cloth 4to. $5.00 net. Postage 35 cents.*
Year Book of 1909:—*Cloth 4to. $5.00 net. Postage 35 cents.*
Year Book of 1910:—*Cloth 4to. $5.00 net. Postage 35 cents.*

WALTER SHAW SPARROW

The English House
How to Judge Its Periods and Styles. *Illustrated. Cloth. 8vo. $2.50 net. Postage 20 cents.*

Hints on House Furnishings
Illustrated. Cloth. 8vo. $2.50 net. Postage 20 cents.
See under International Studio Extra Numbers.

J. H. ELDER-DUNCAN

The House Beautiful and Useful
Being Practical Suggestions on Furnishing and Decoration. *Large 4to. Cloth. $3.50 net. Express 35 cents.*

Country Cottages and Week-end Homes
Numerous Illustrations and Plans of Cottages by well-known Architects. *Large 4to. Cloth bound. $3.50 net. Express 35 cents.*

CHARLES GOURLAY

The Construction of a House
A Text Book for Architects, Builders, Craftsmen and Students. *Forty Plates. Cloth. 4to. $2.75 net. Postage 25 cents.*